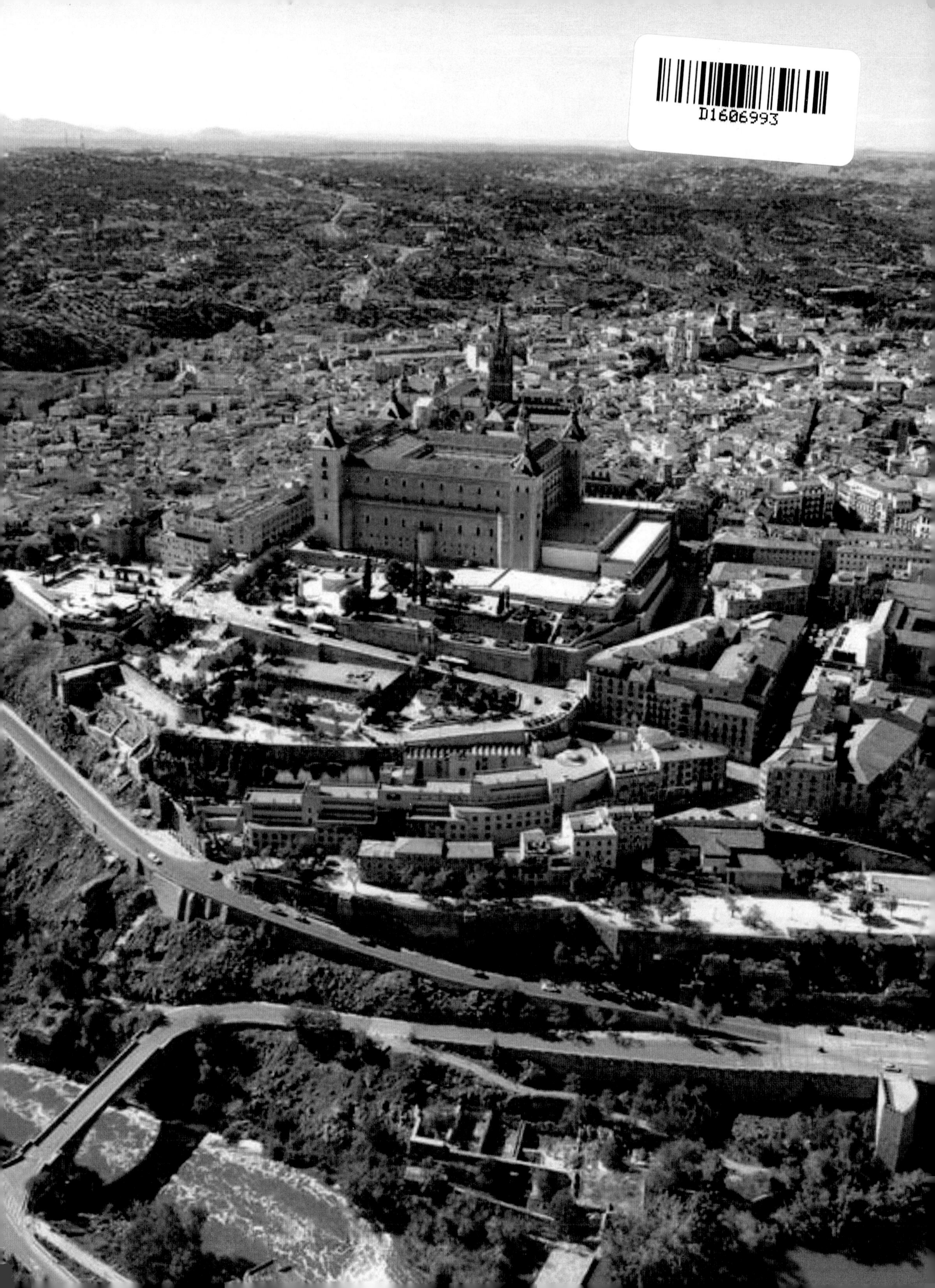

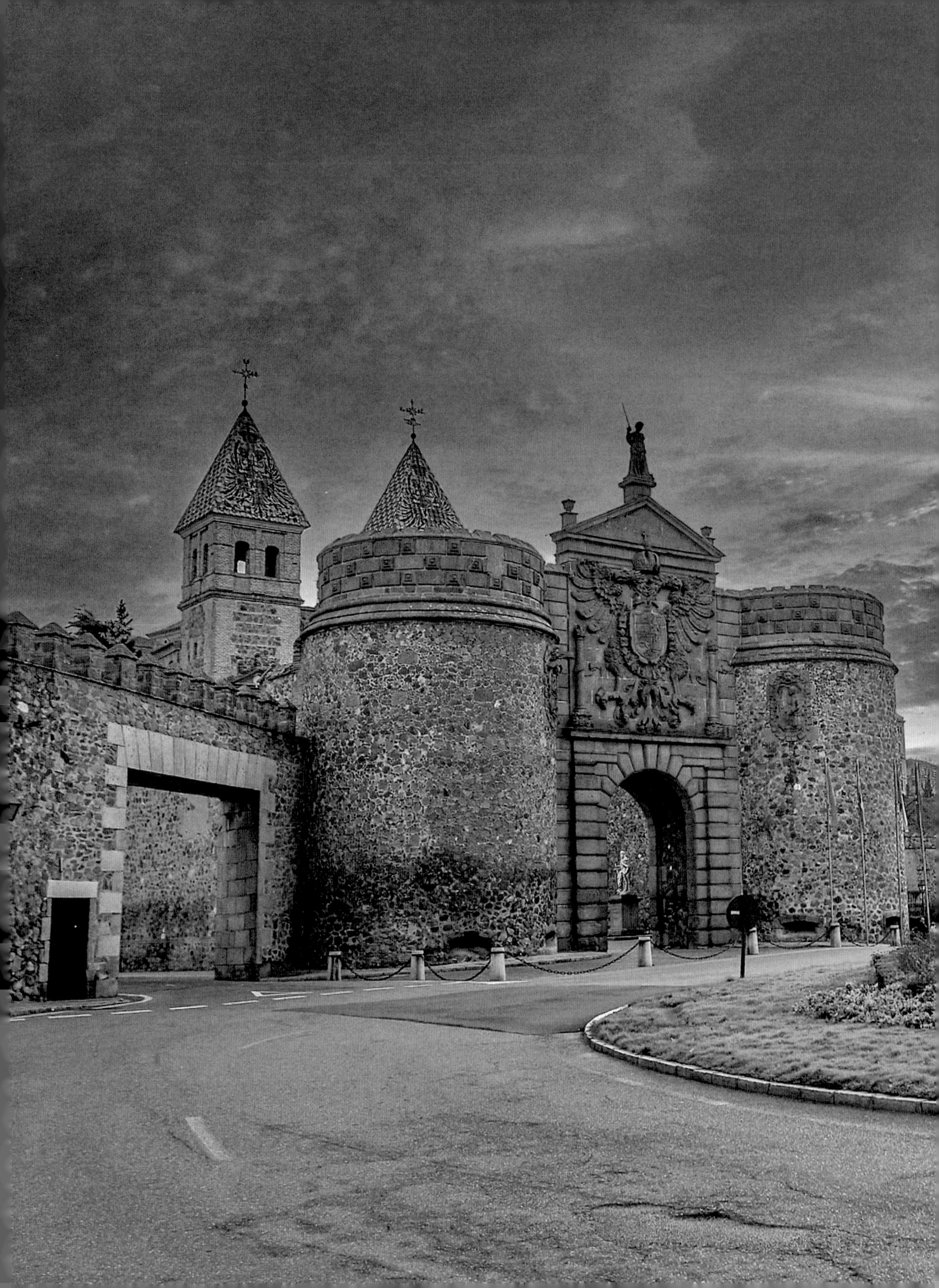

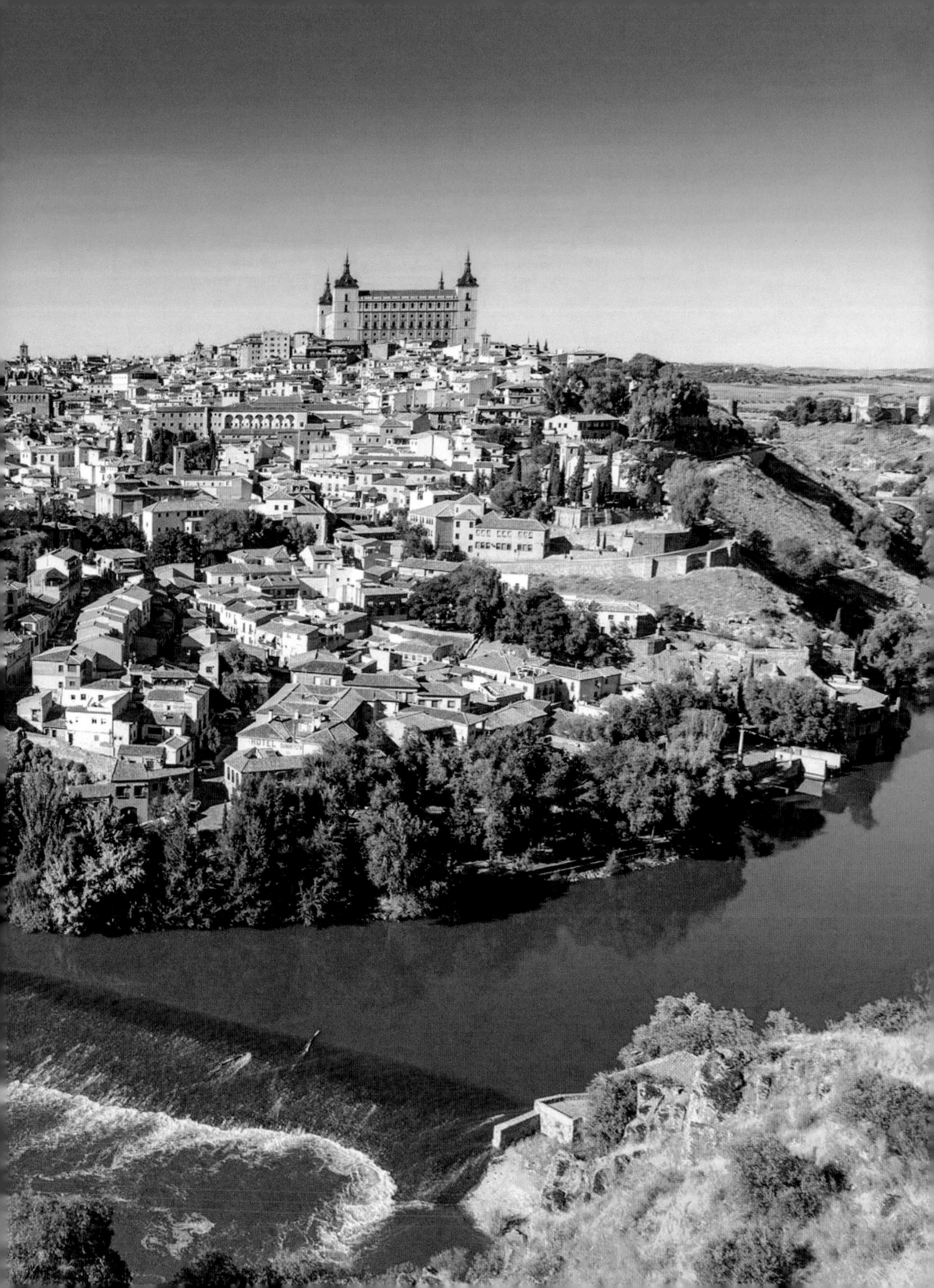
HOTEL

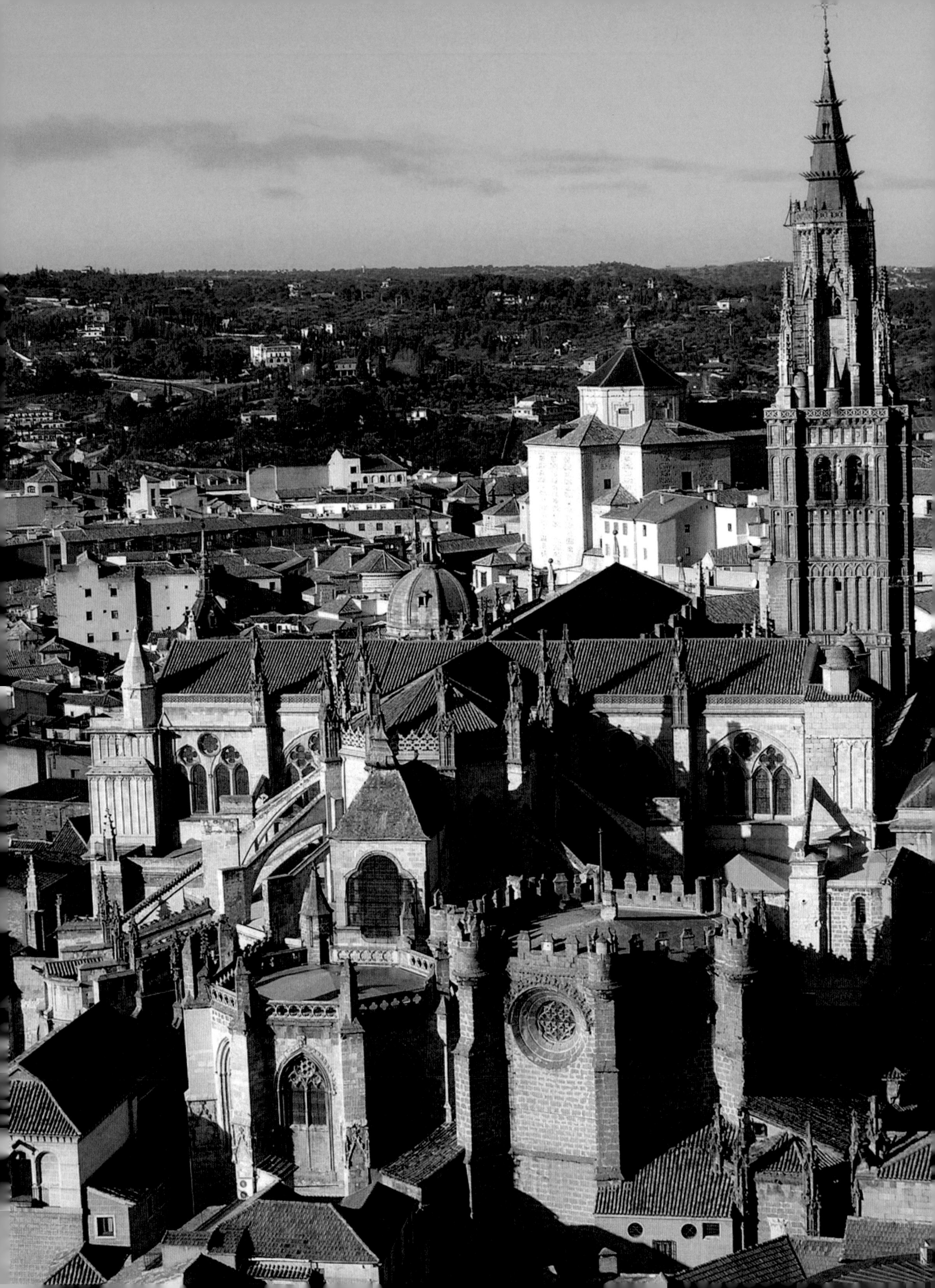

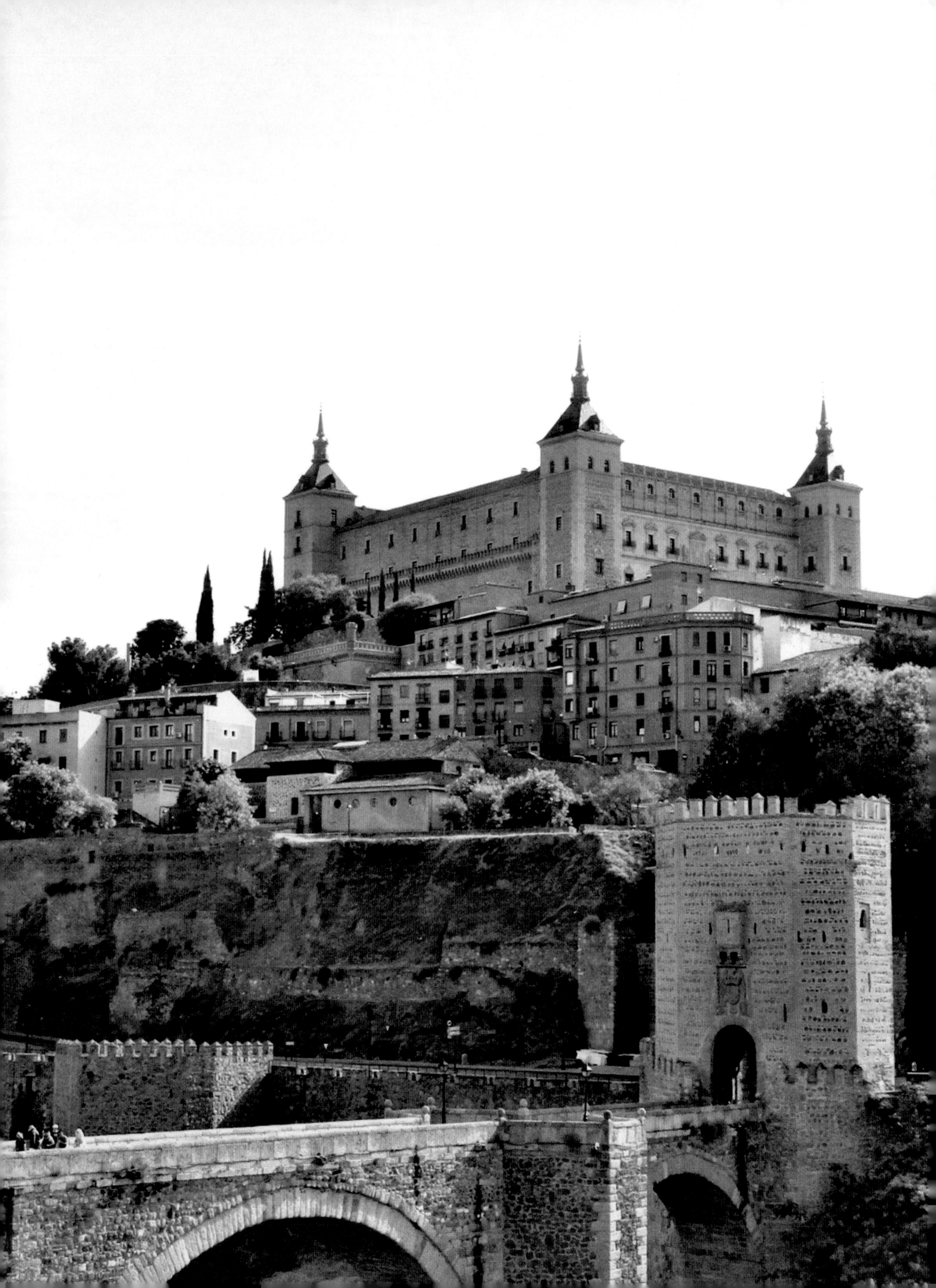

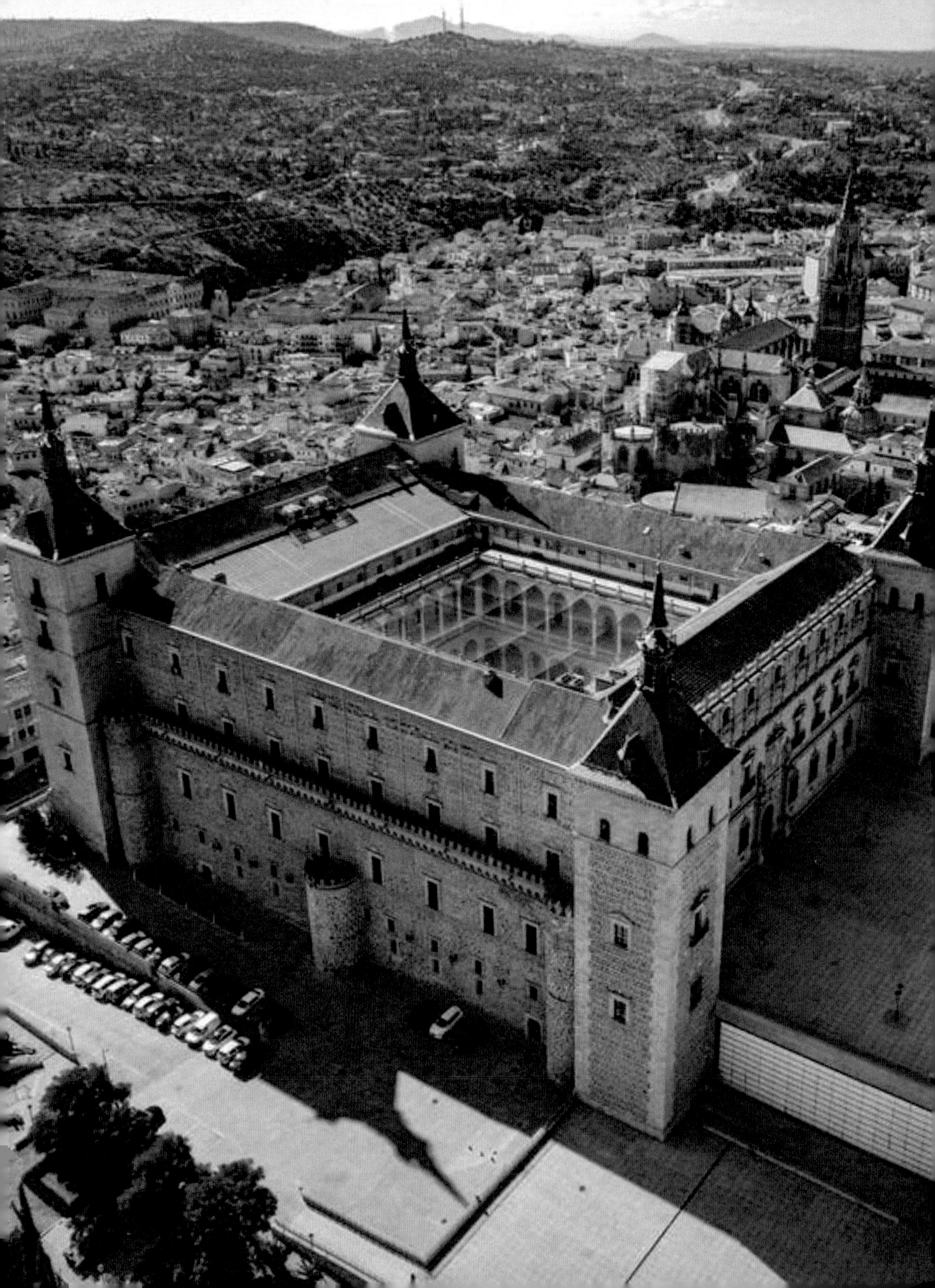

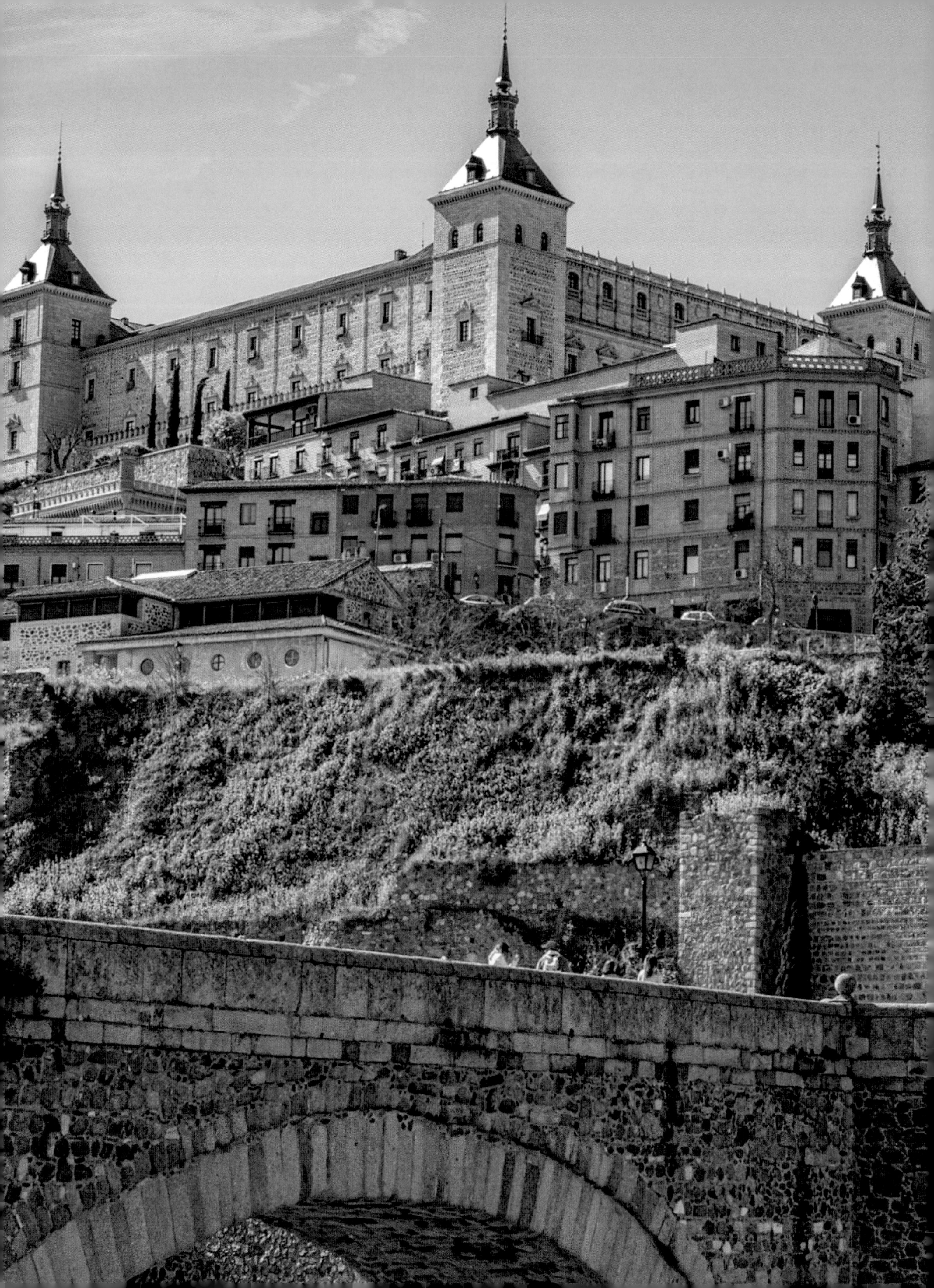

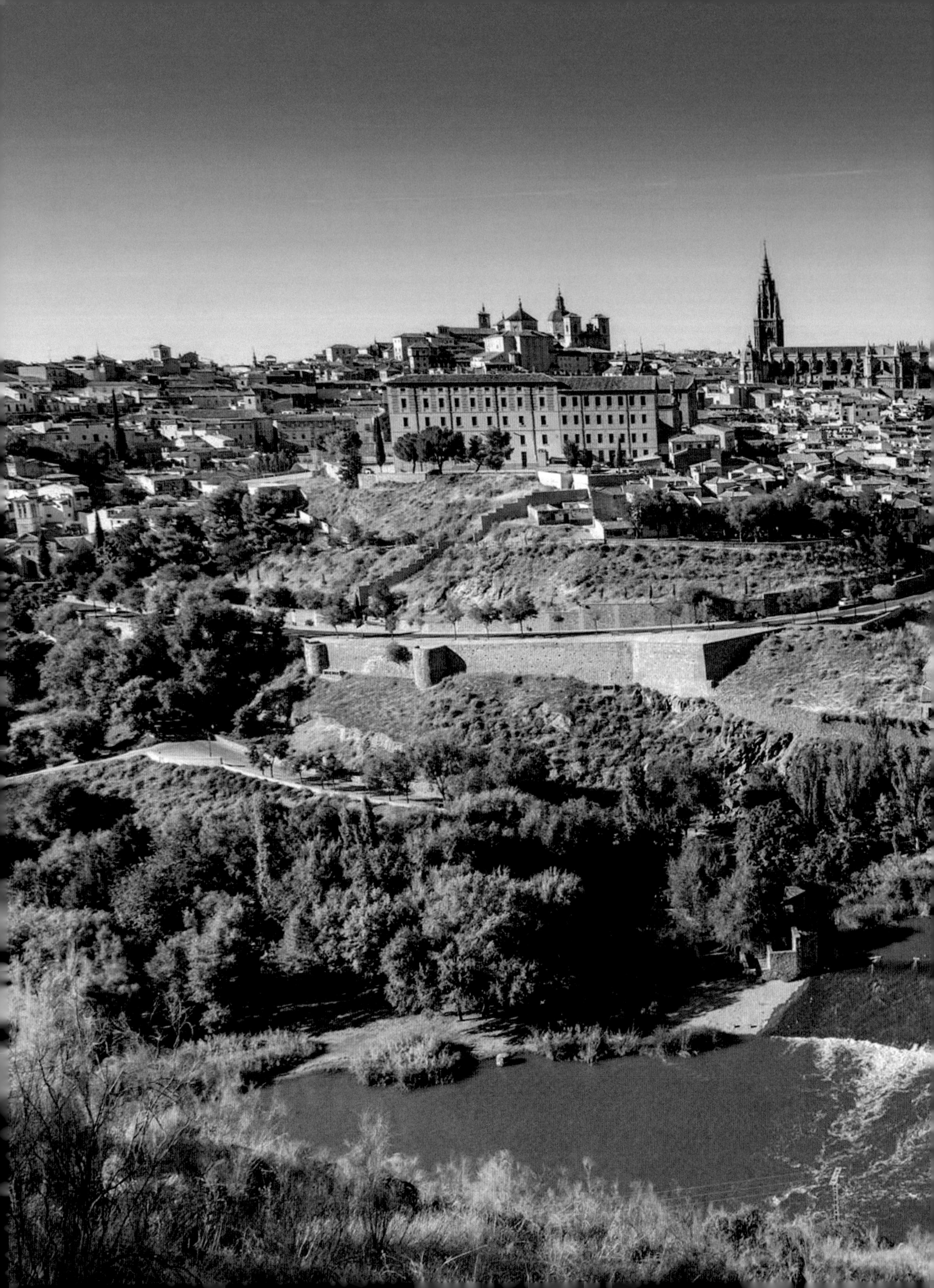

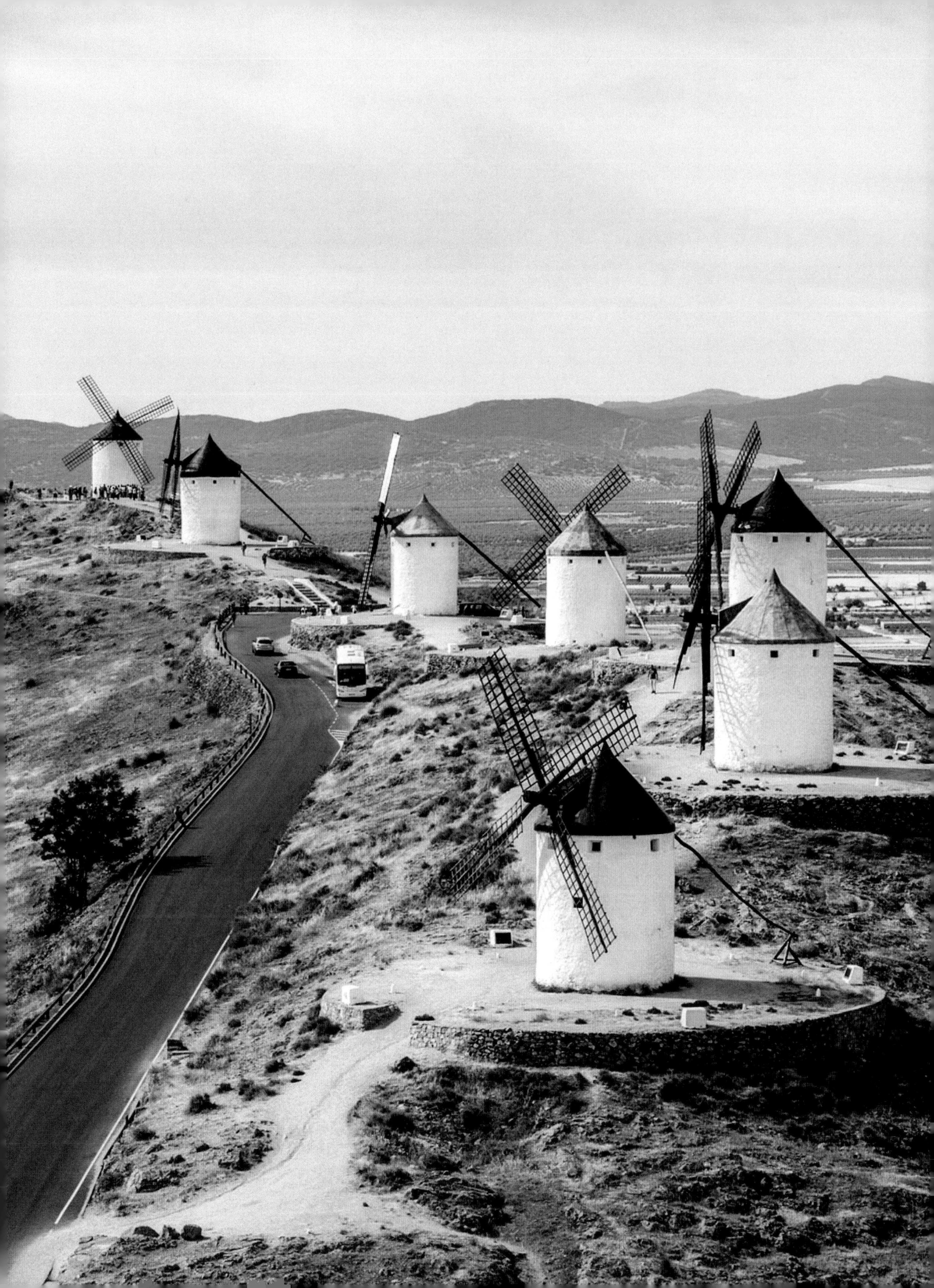

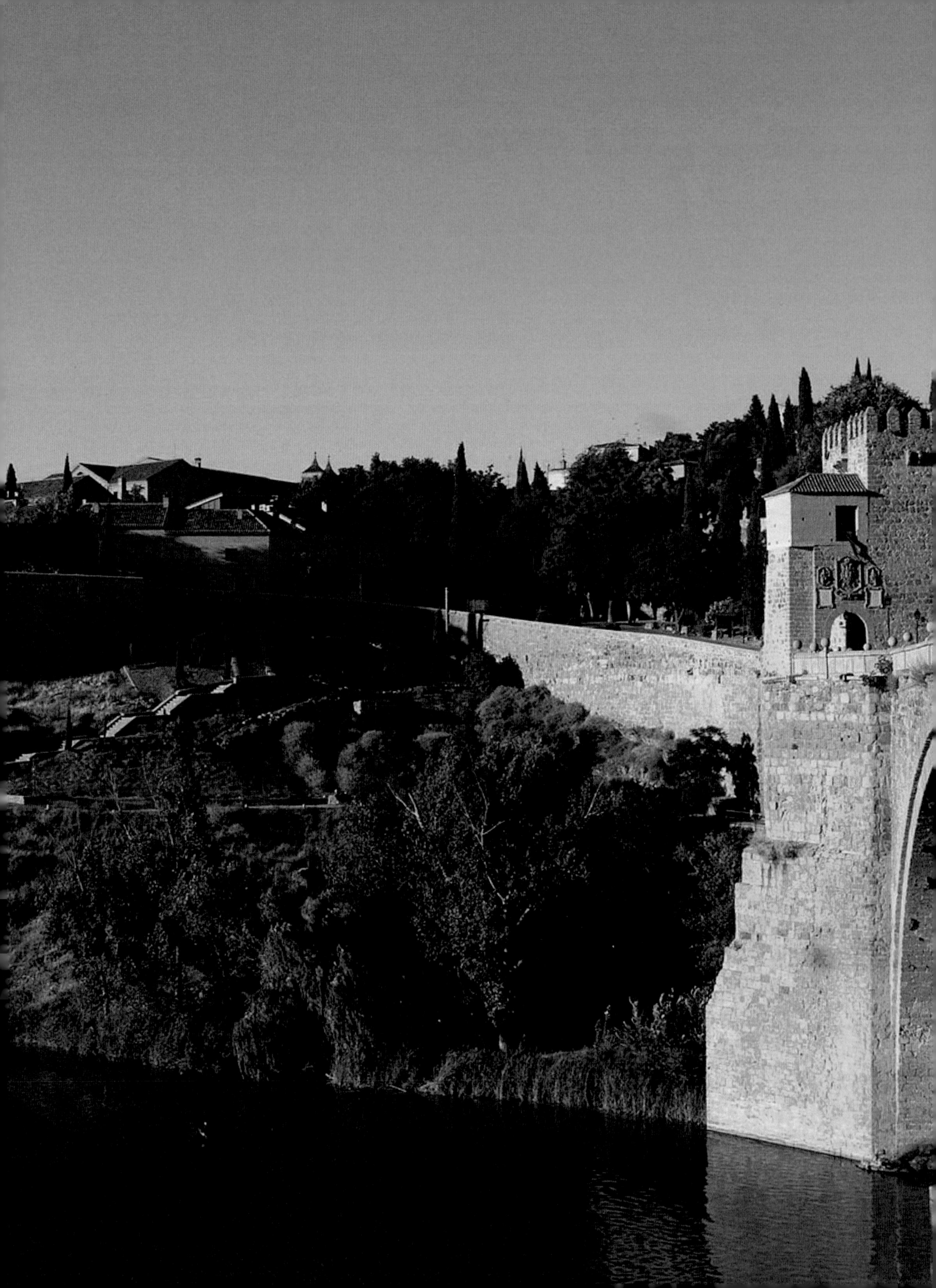

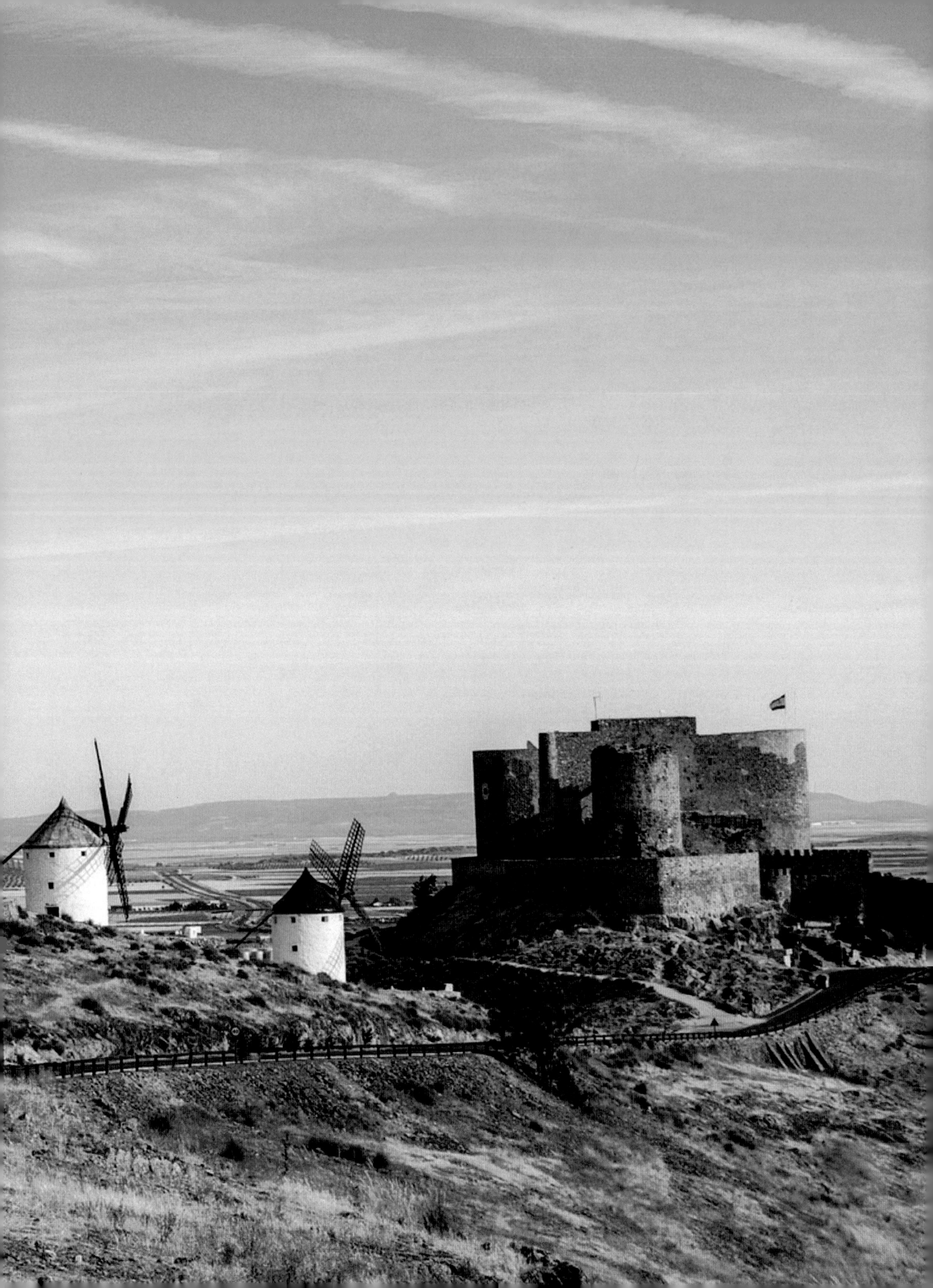

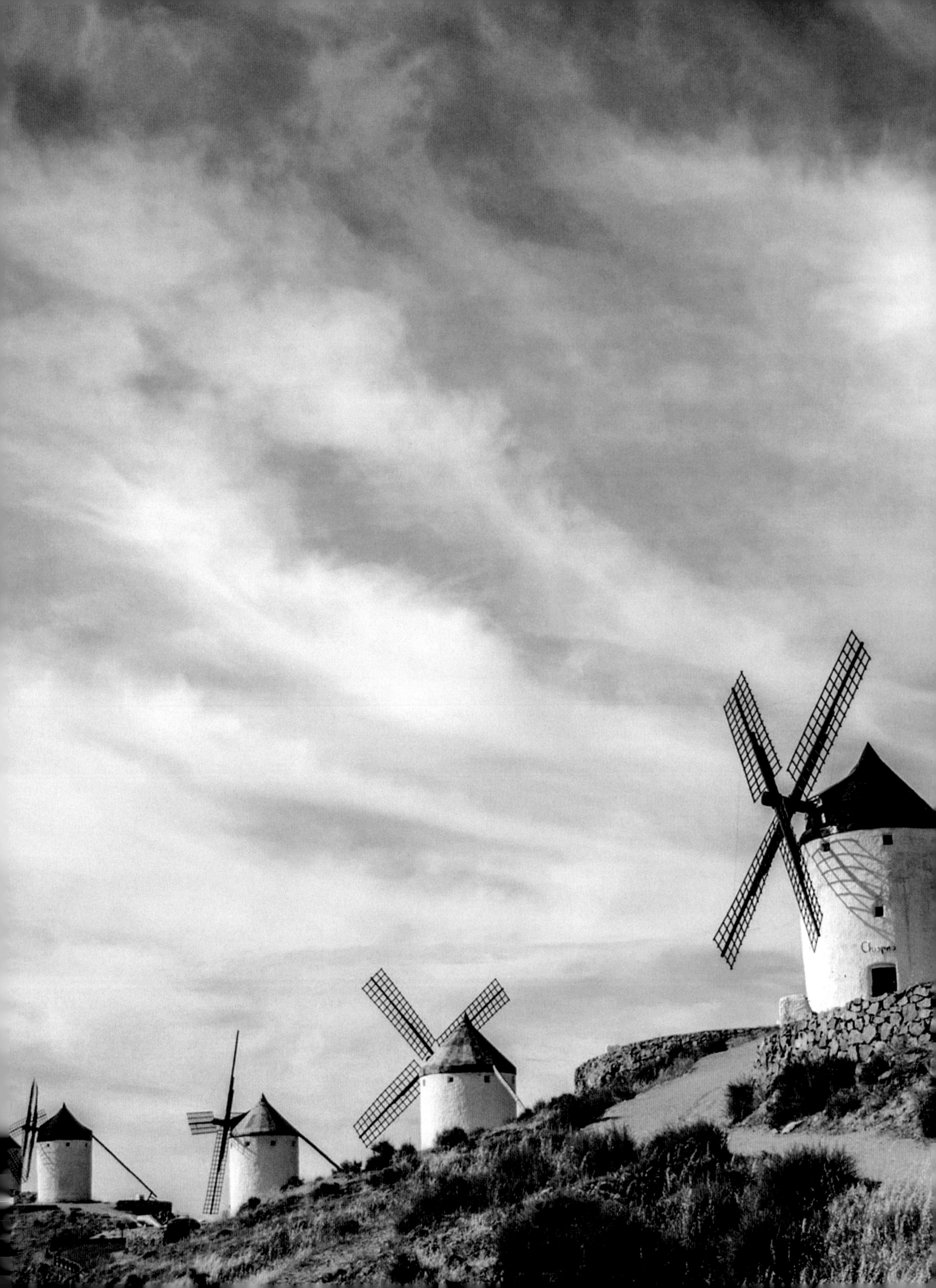

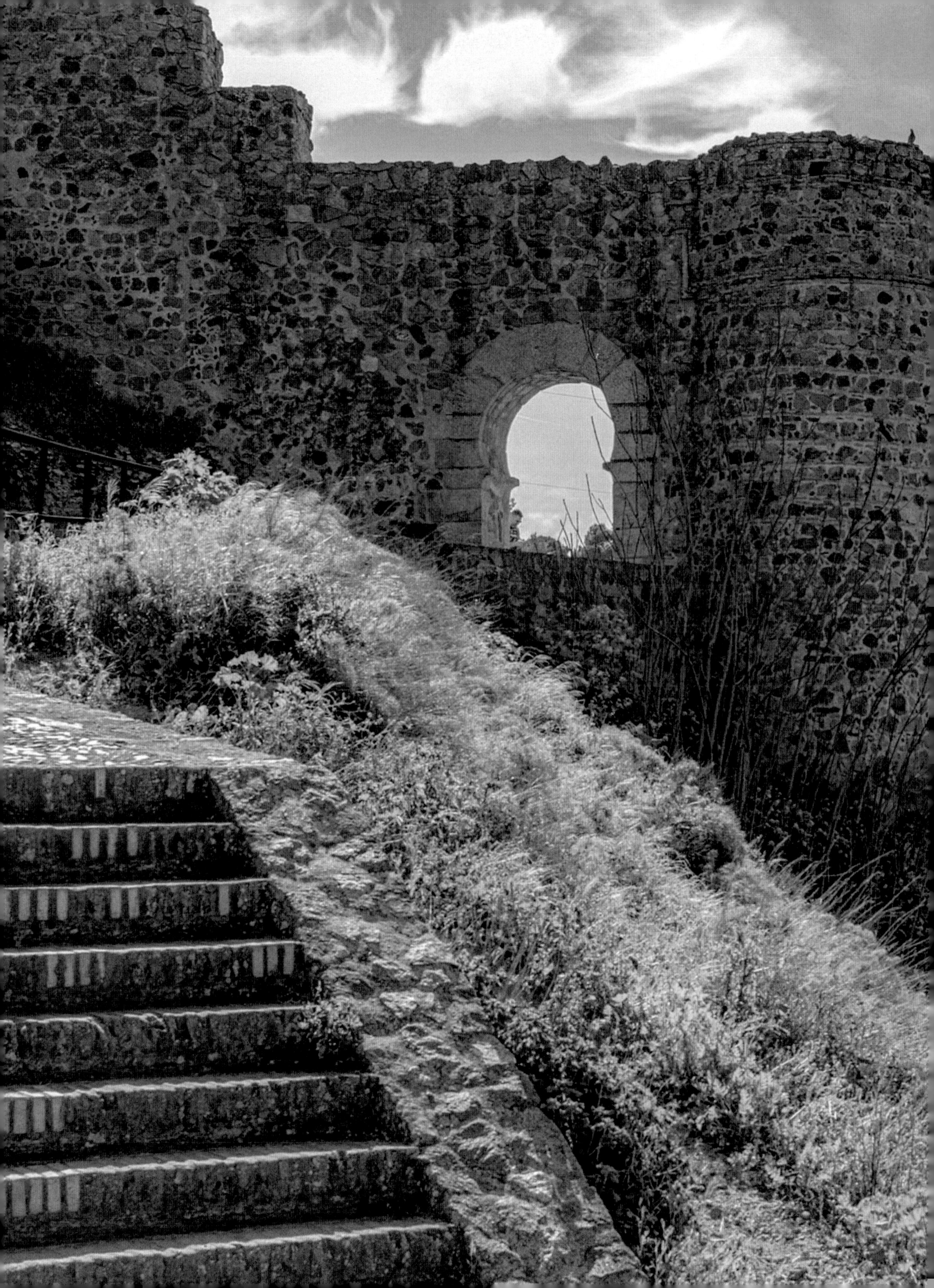

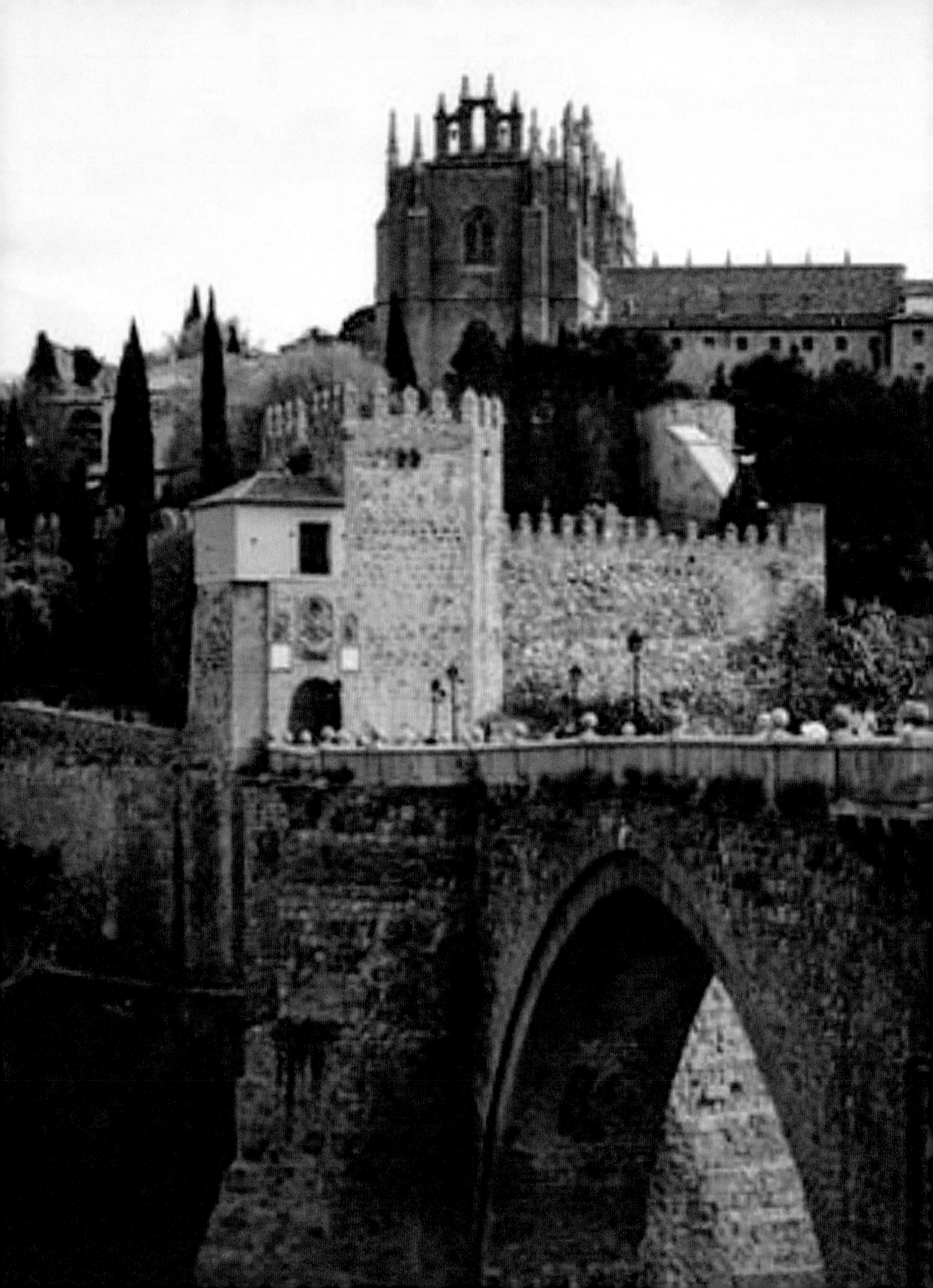

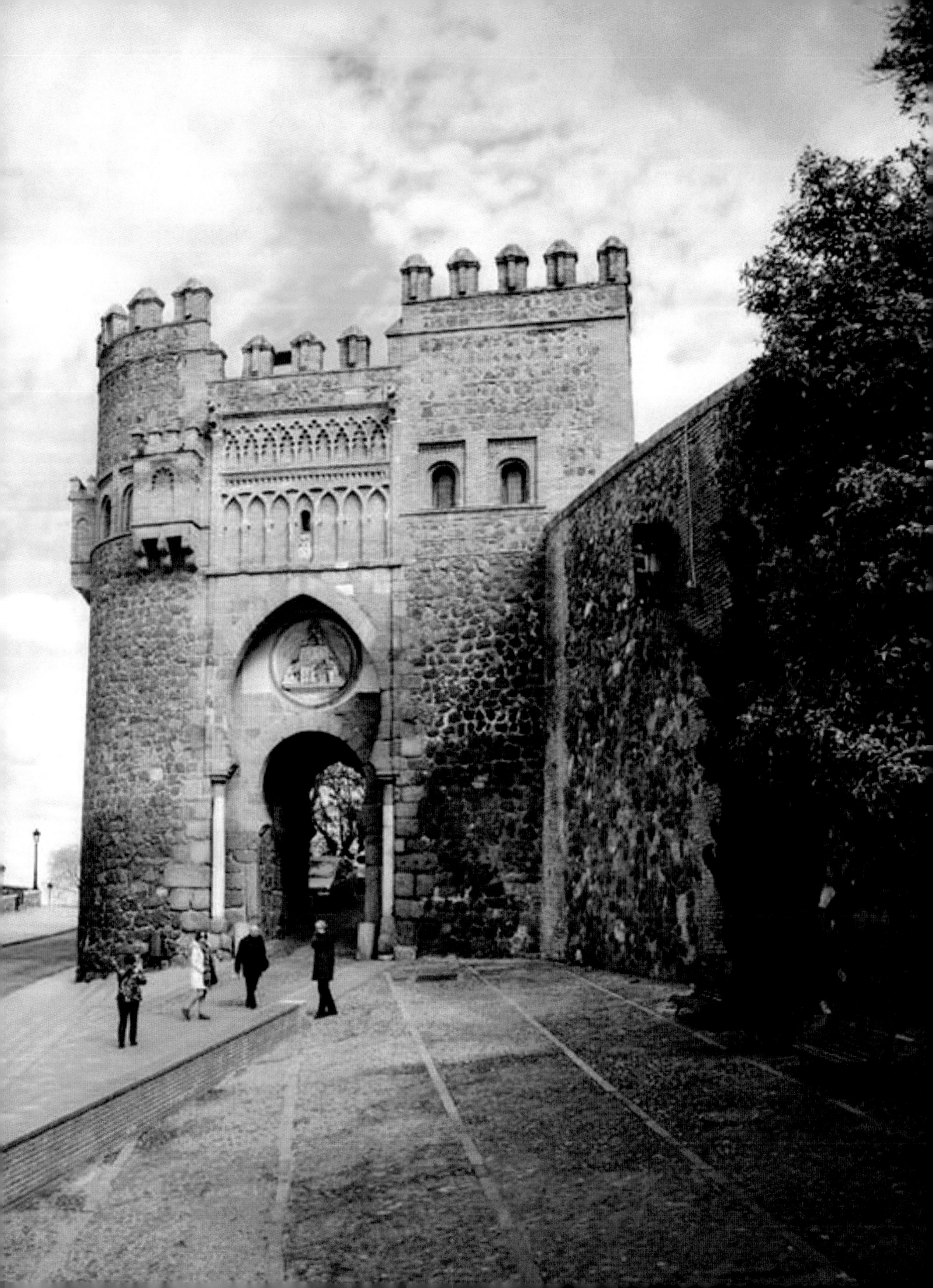

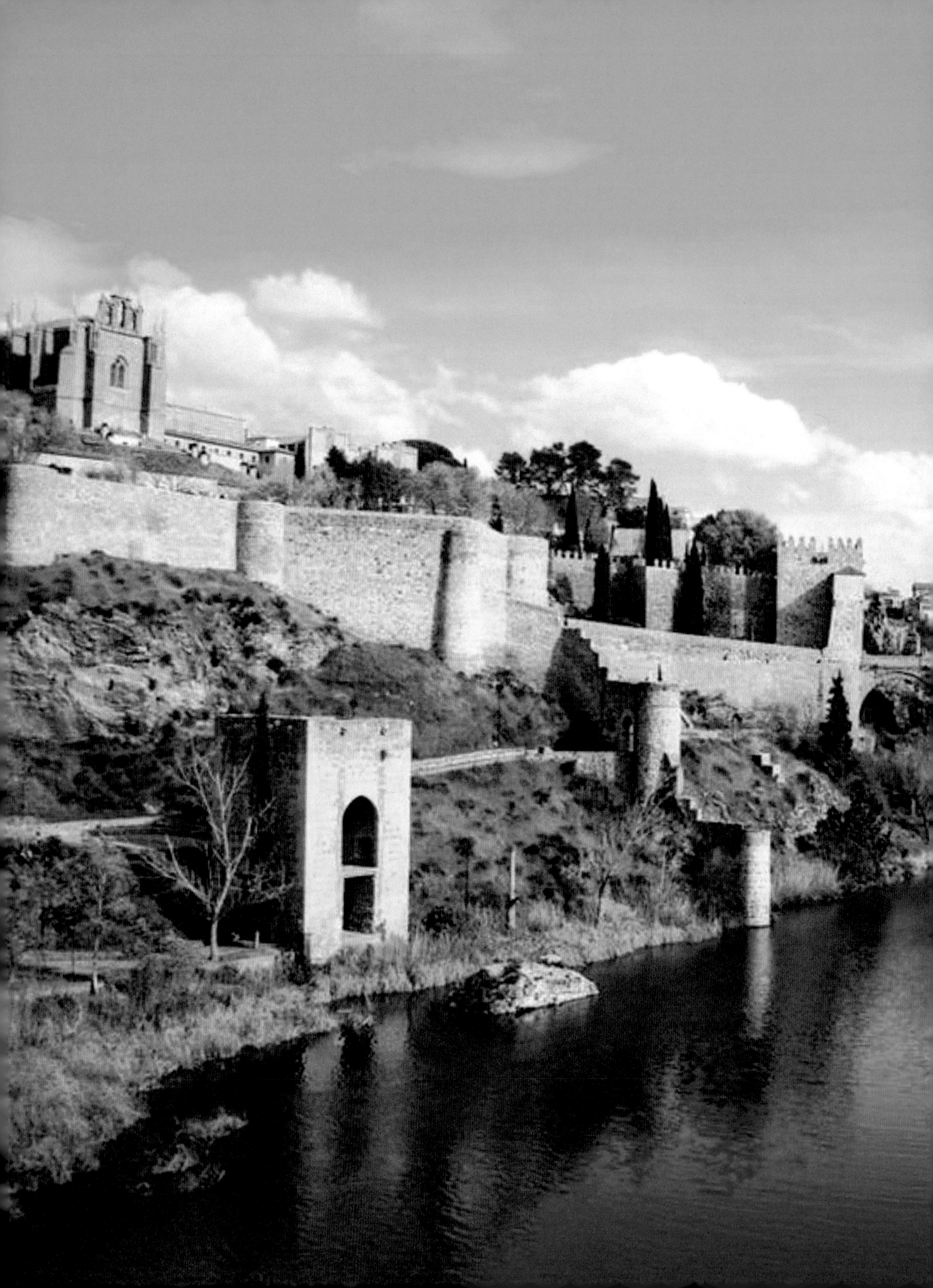

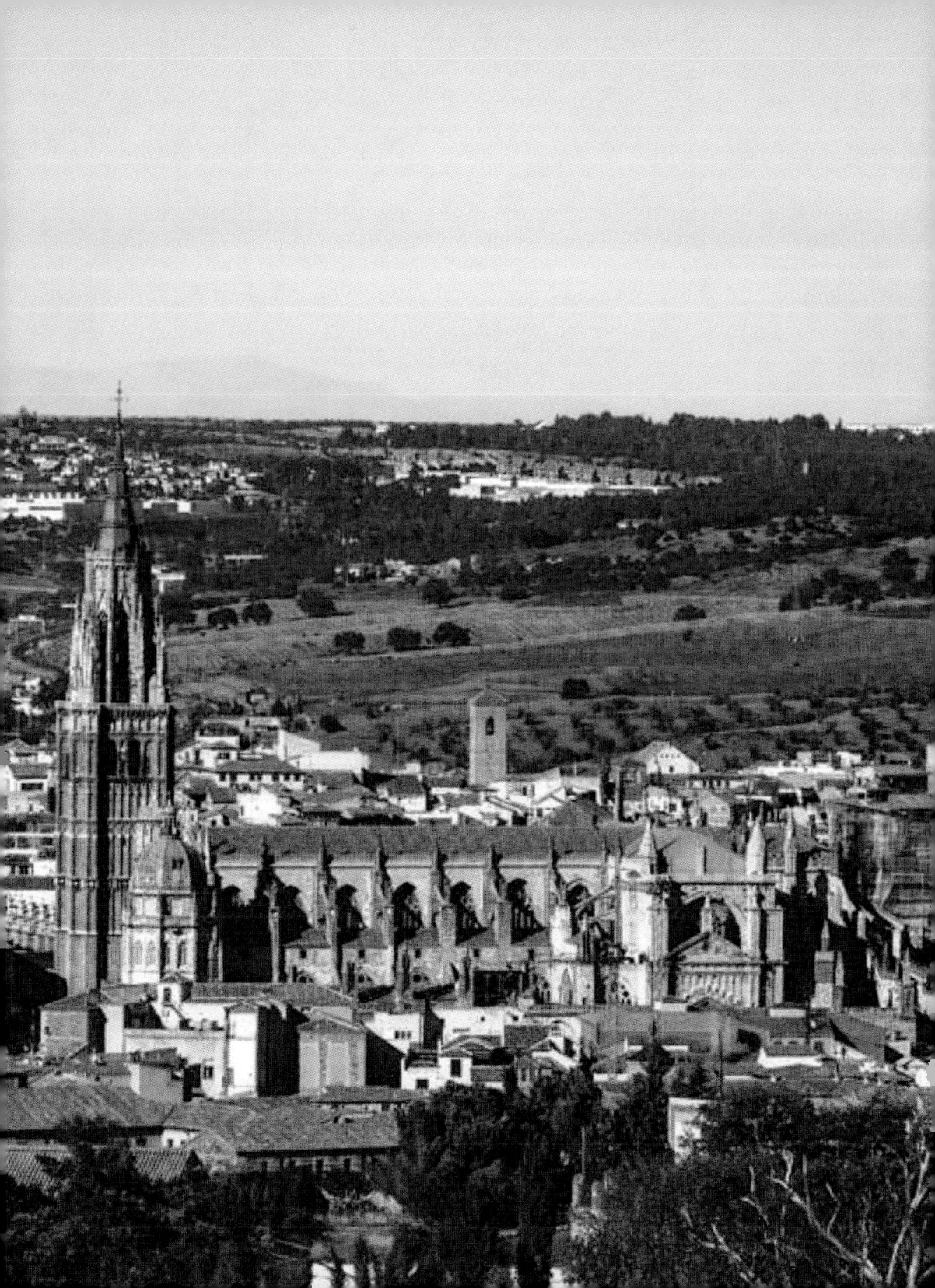

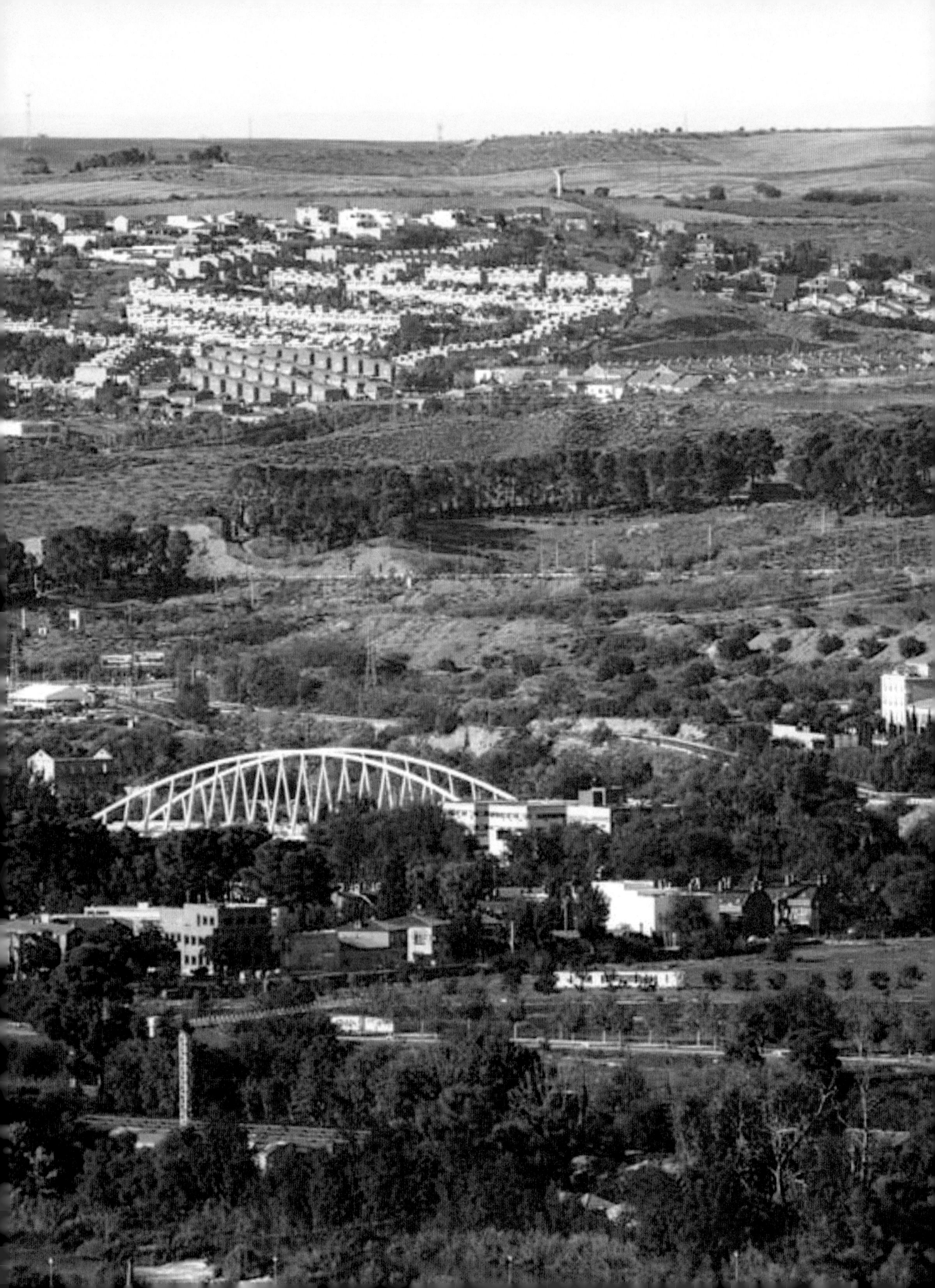

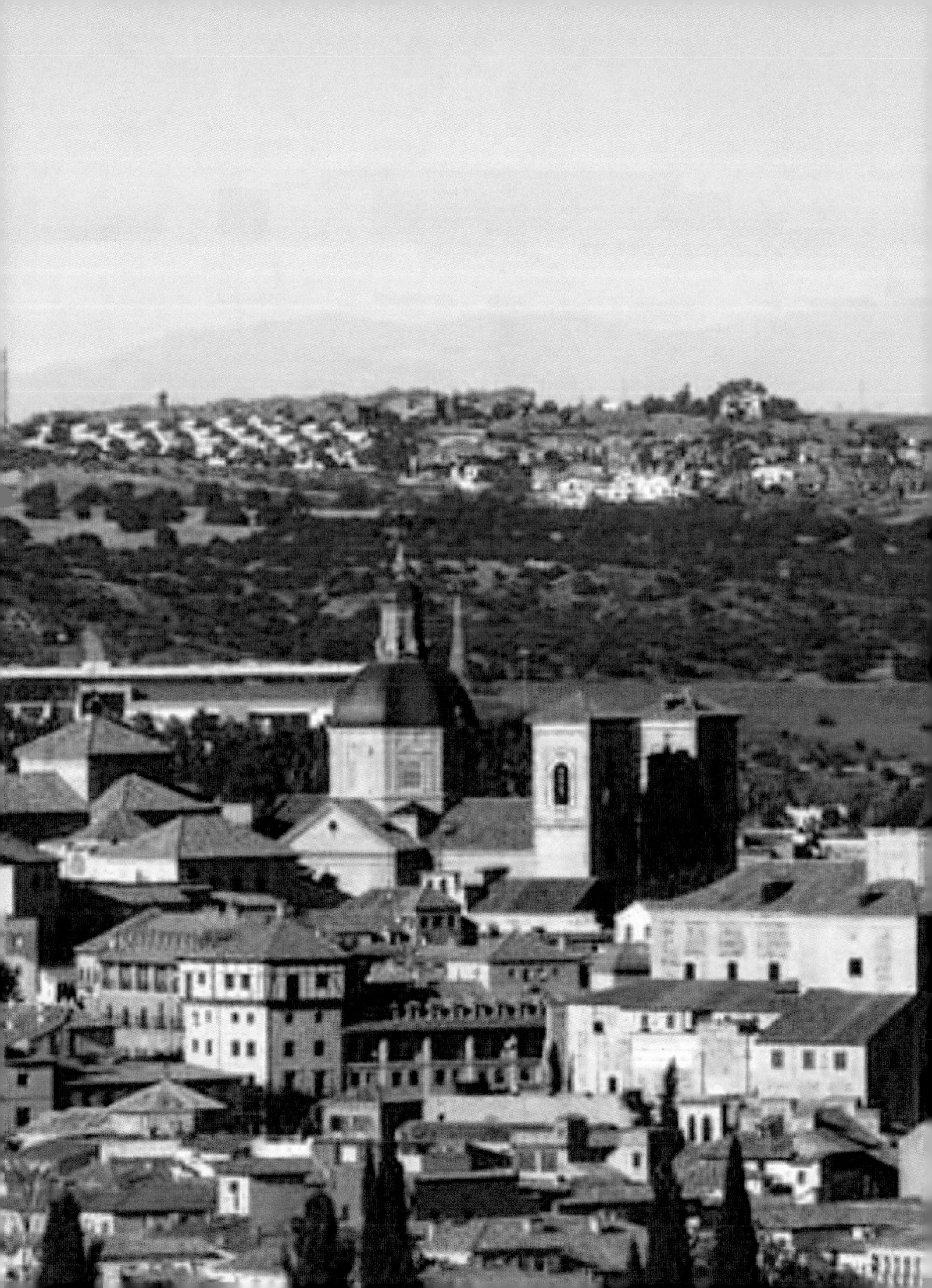

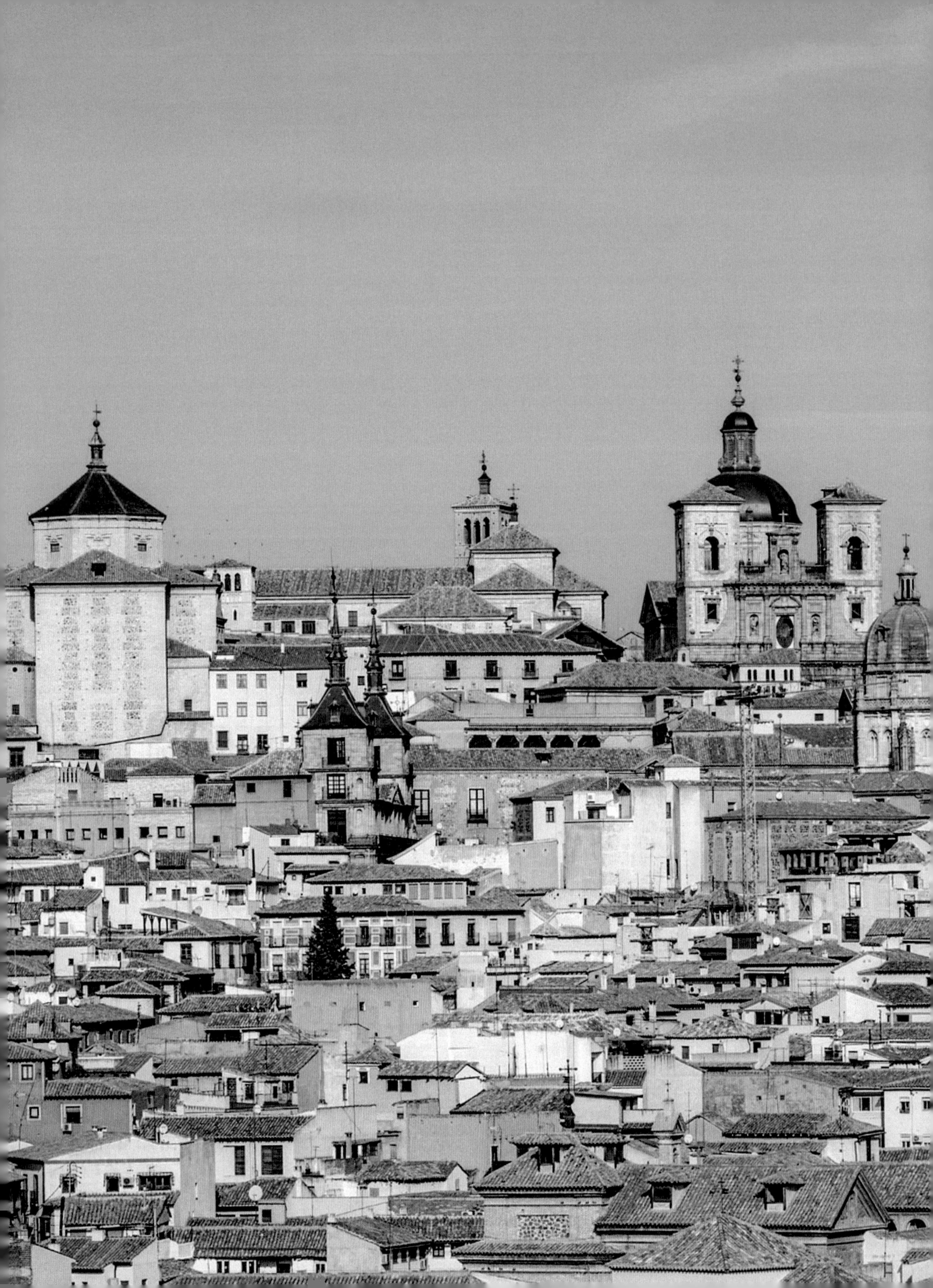

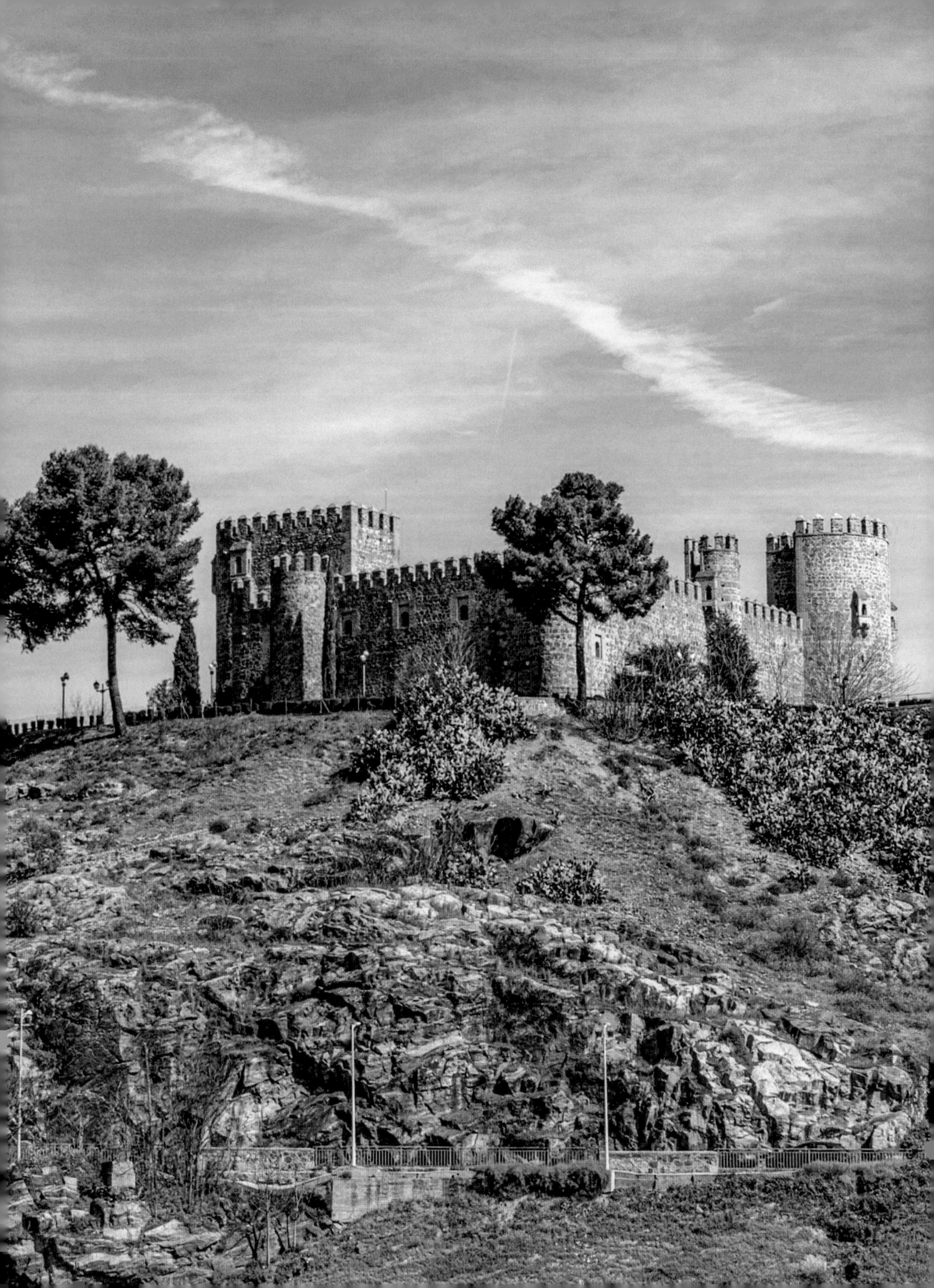

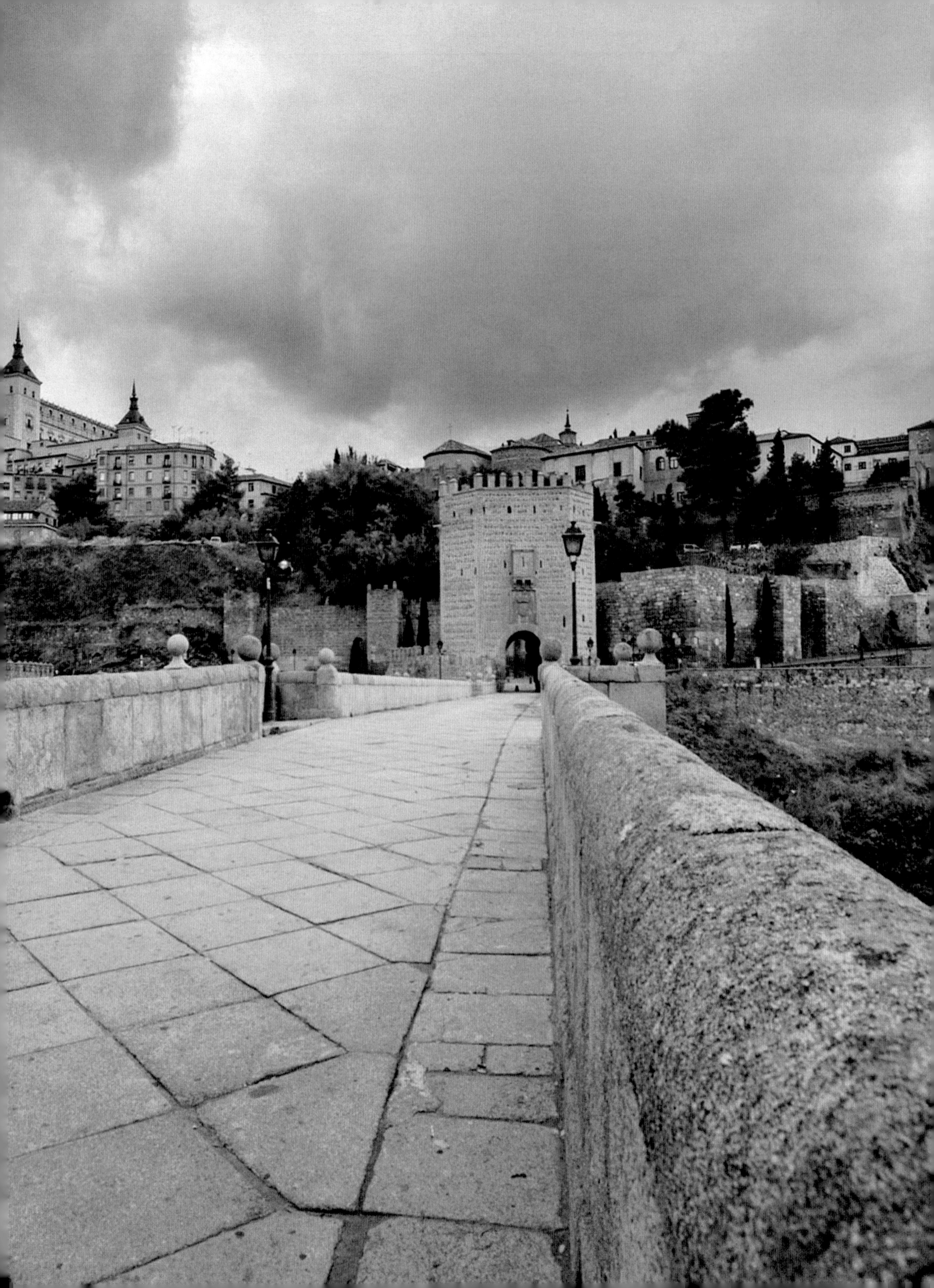

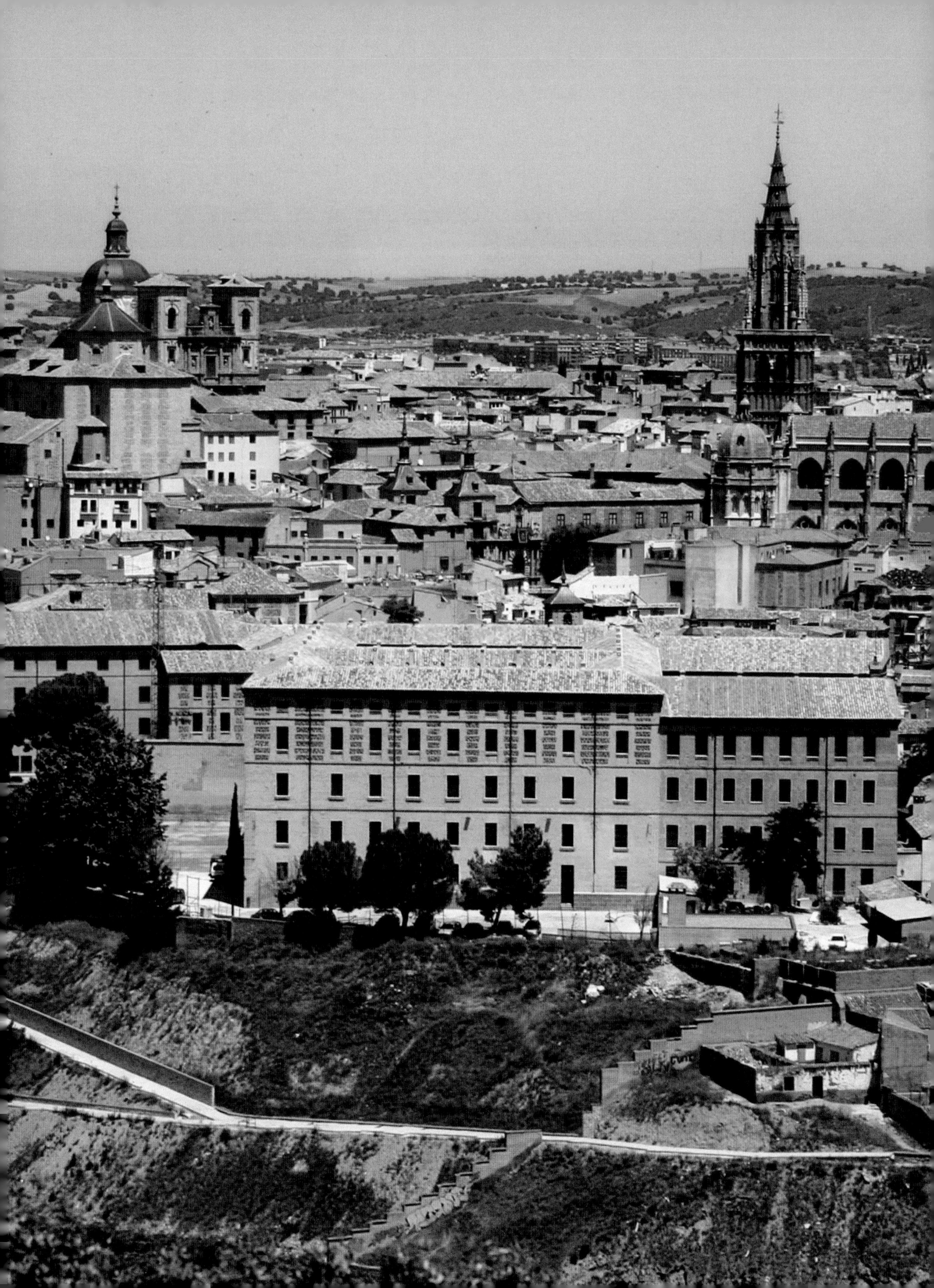

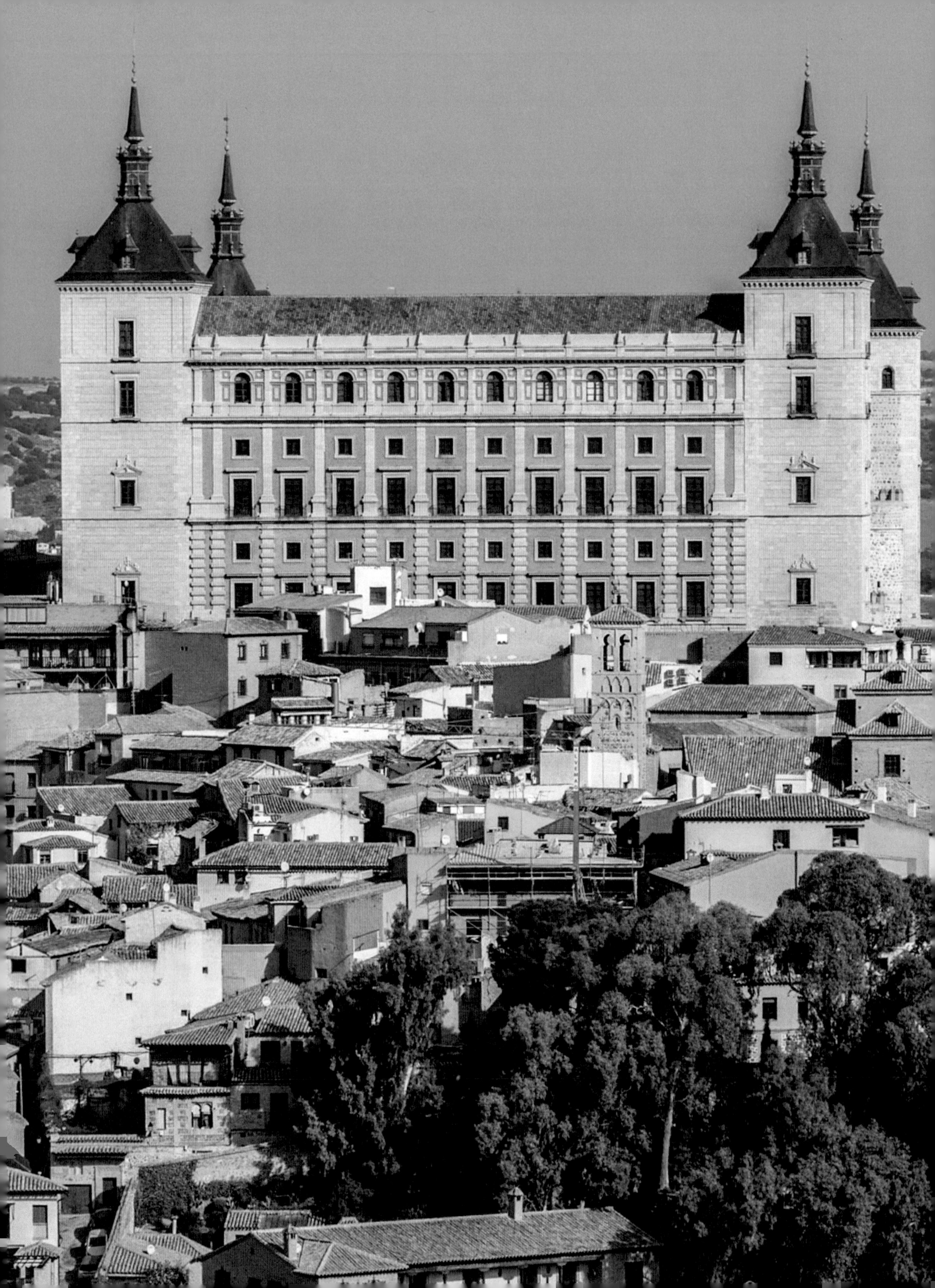

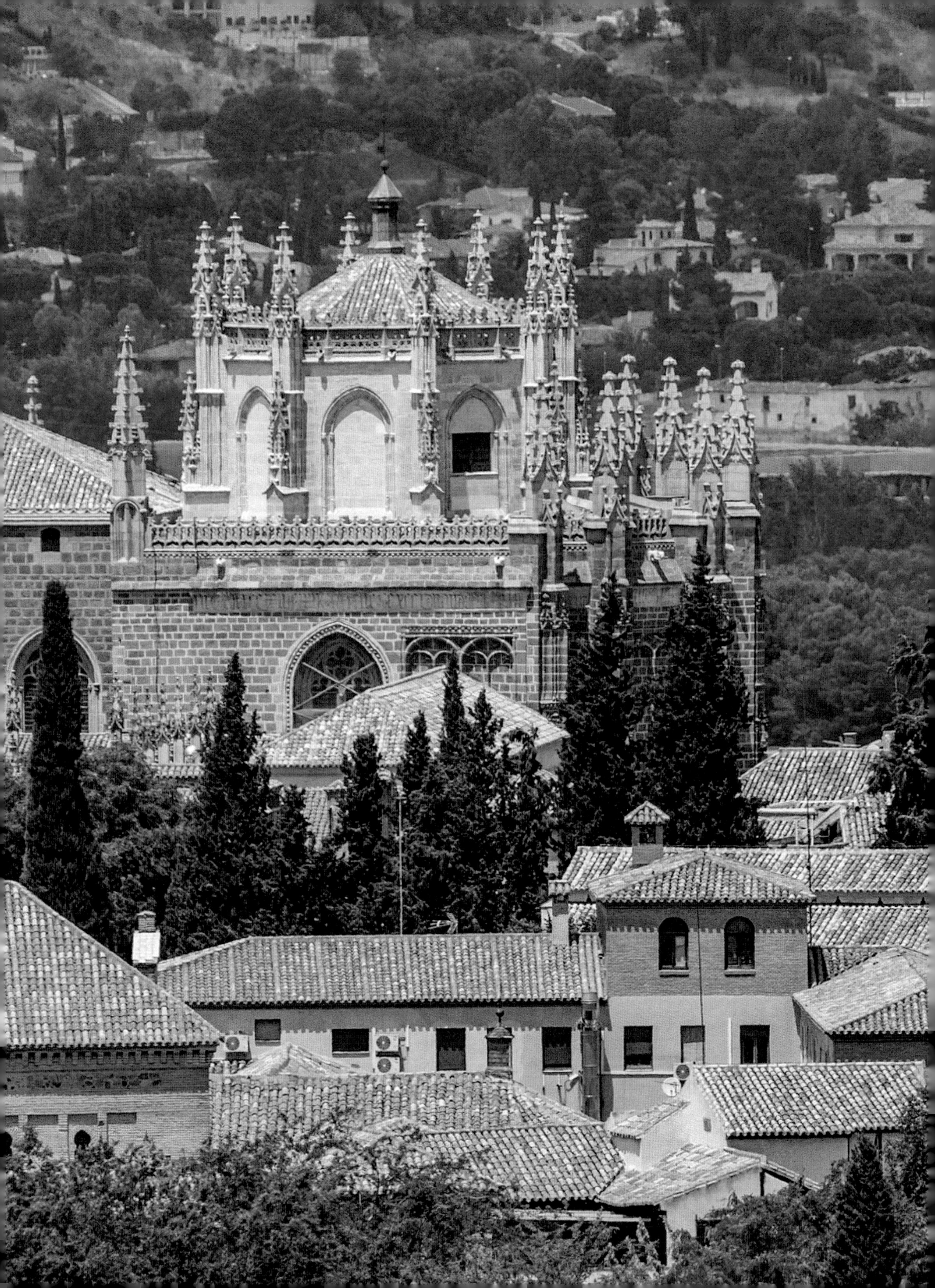

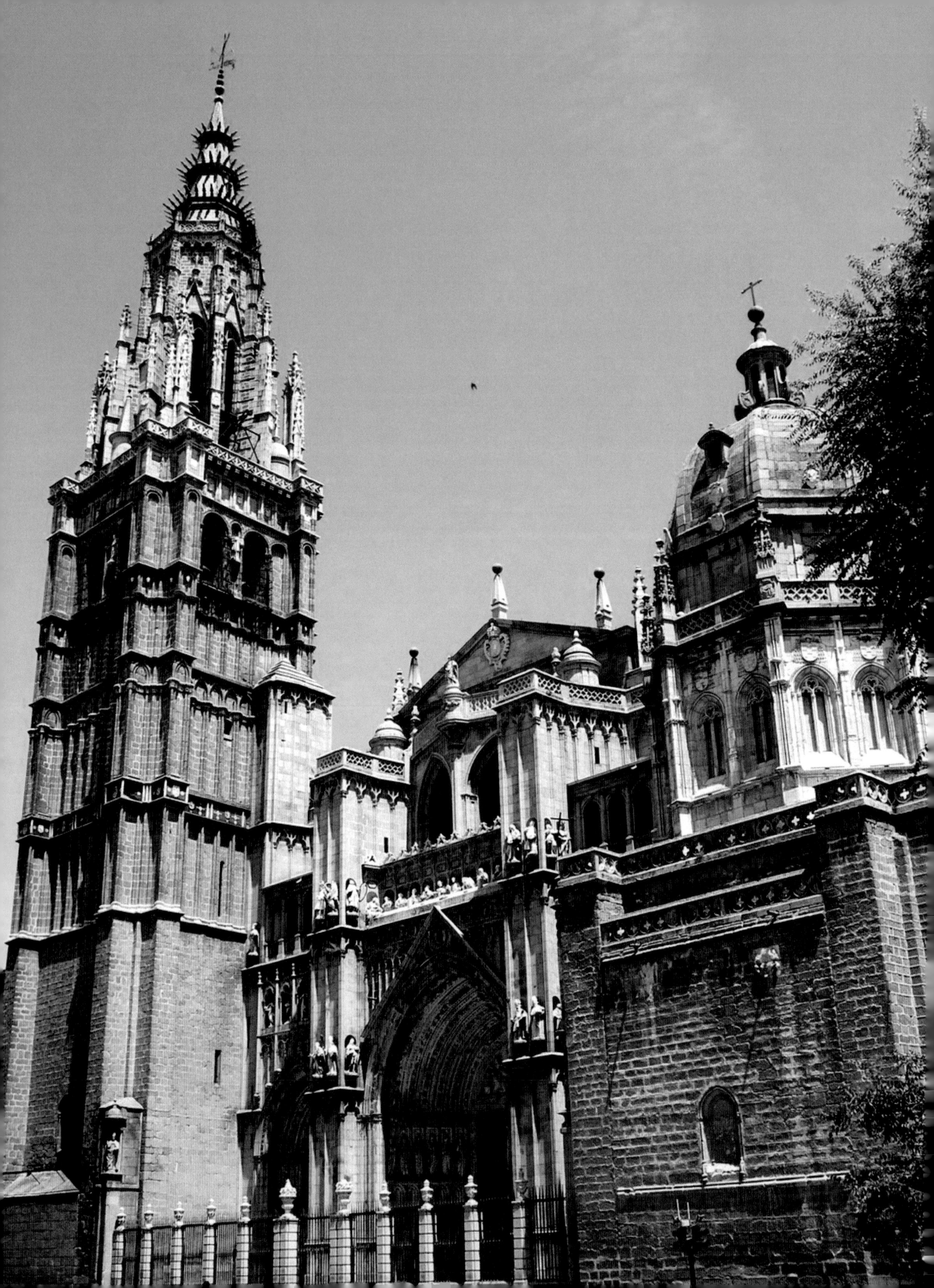

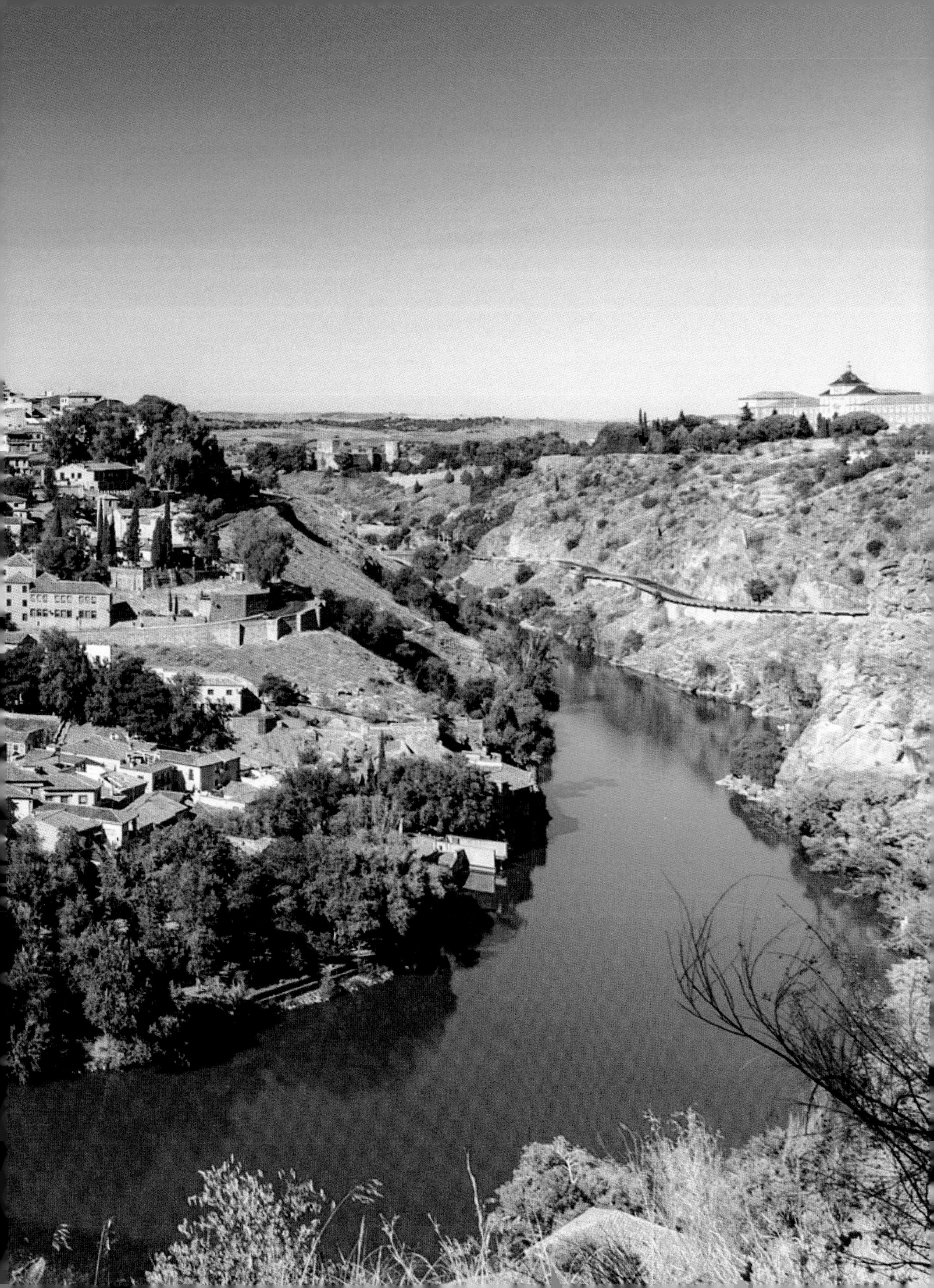

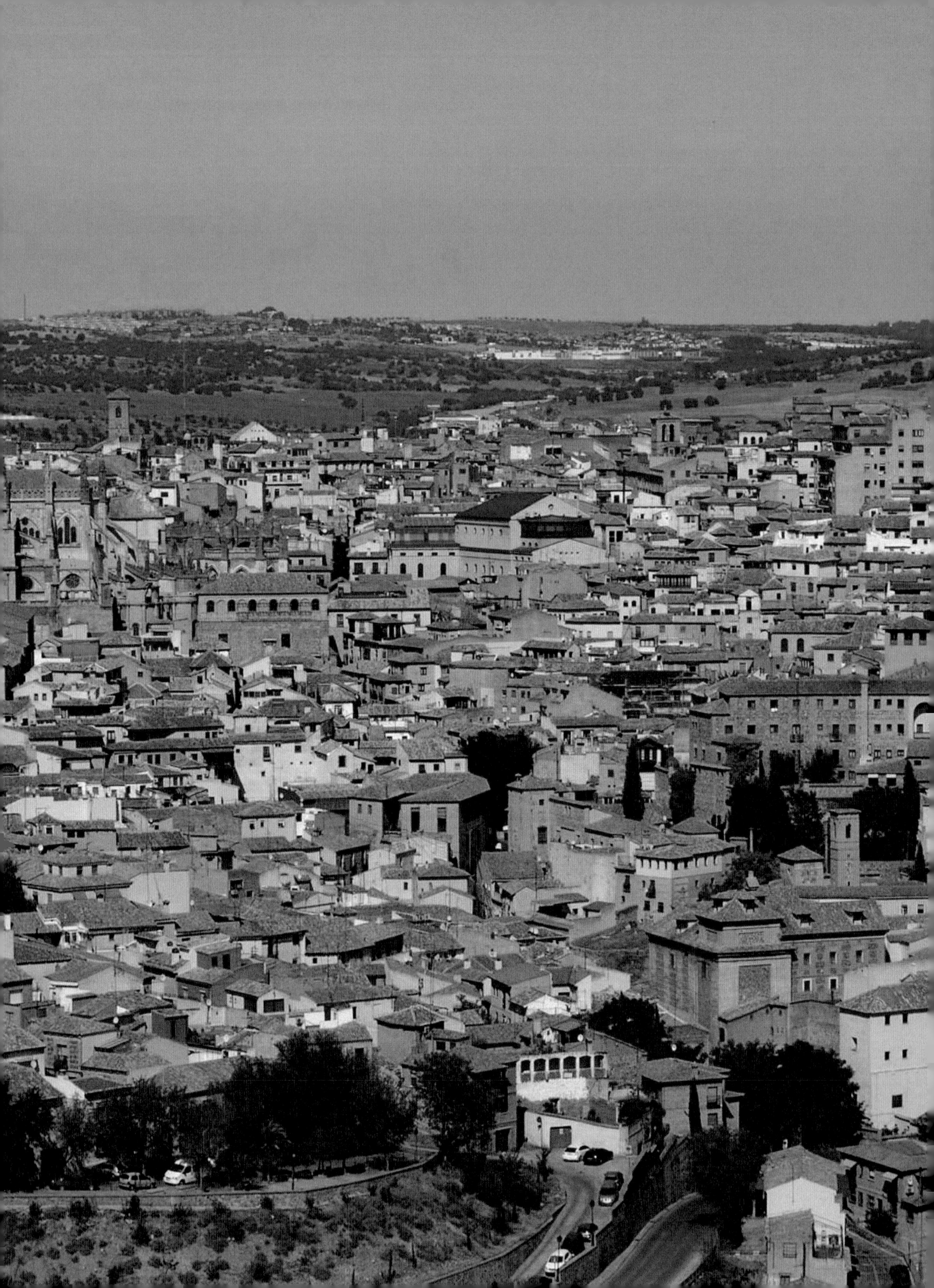

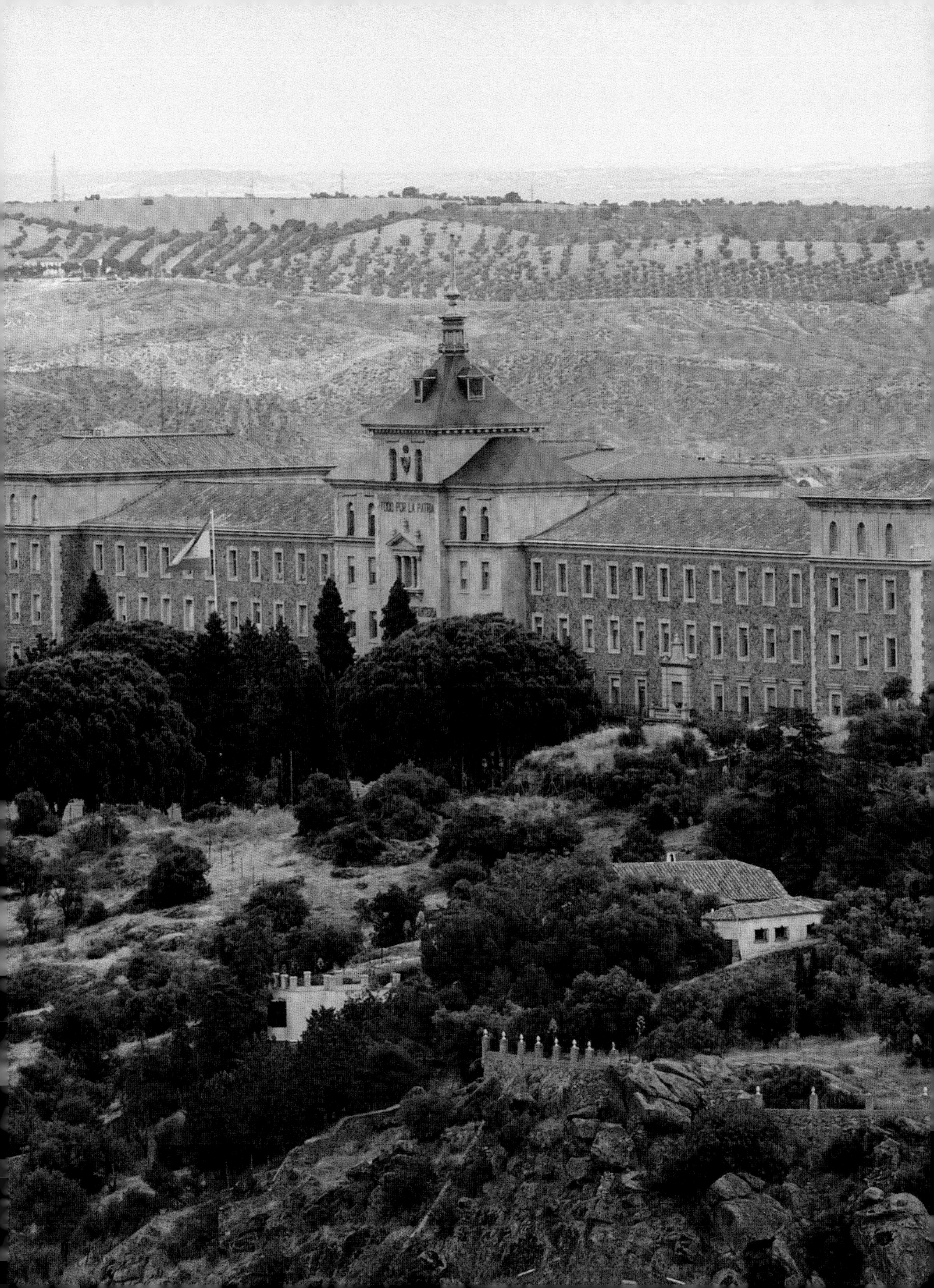
TODO POR LA PATRIA

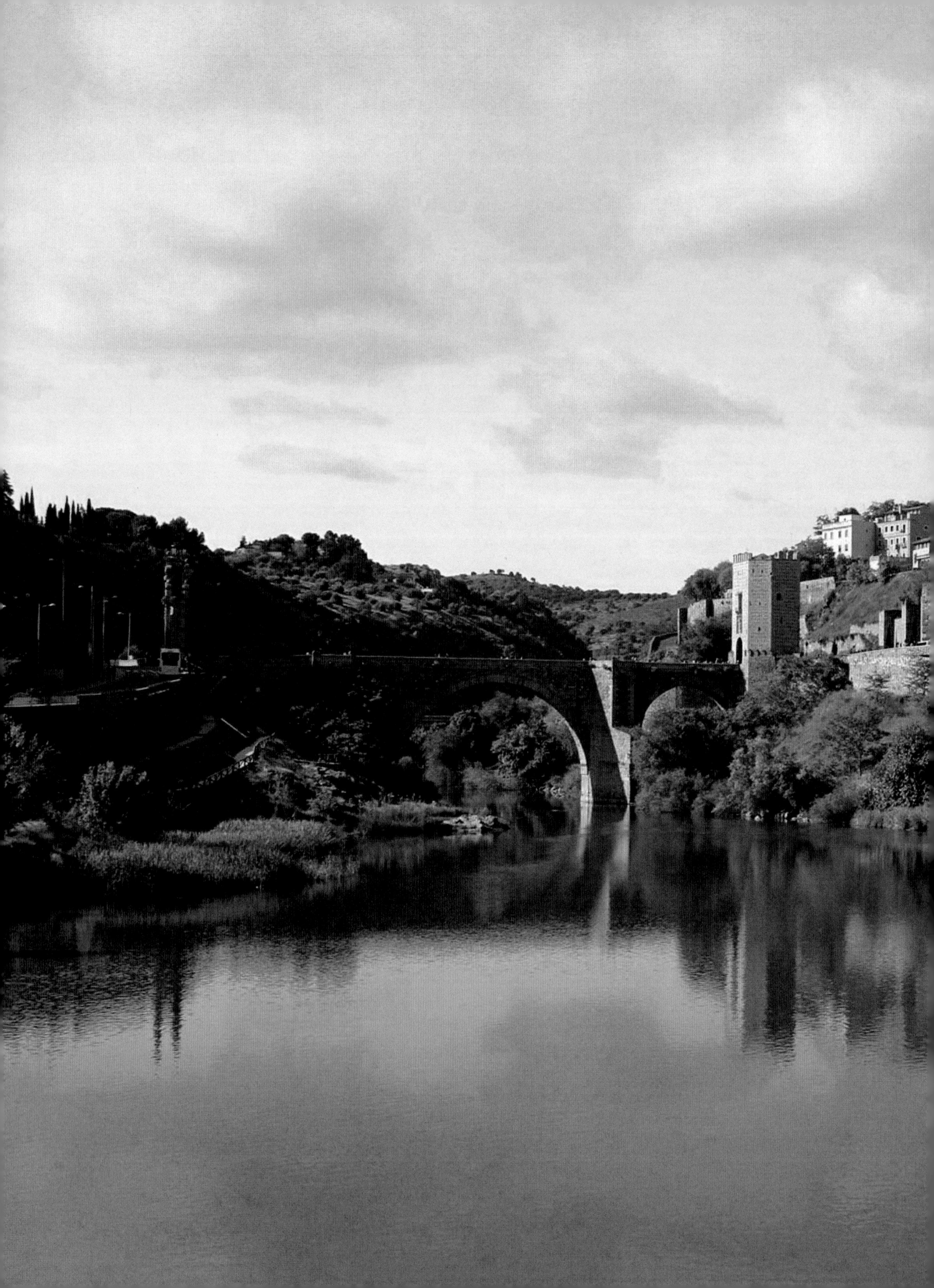

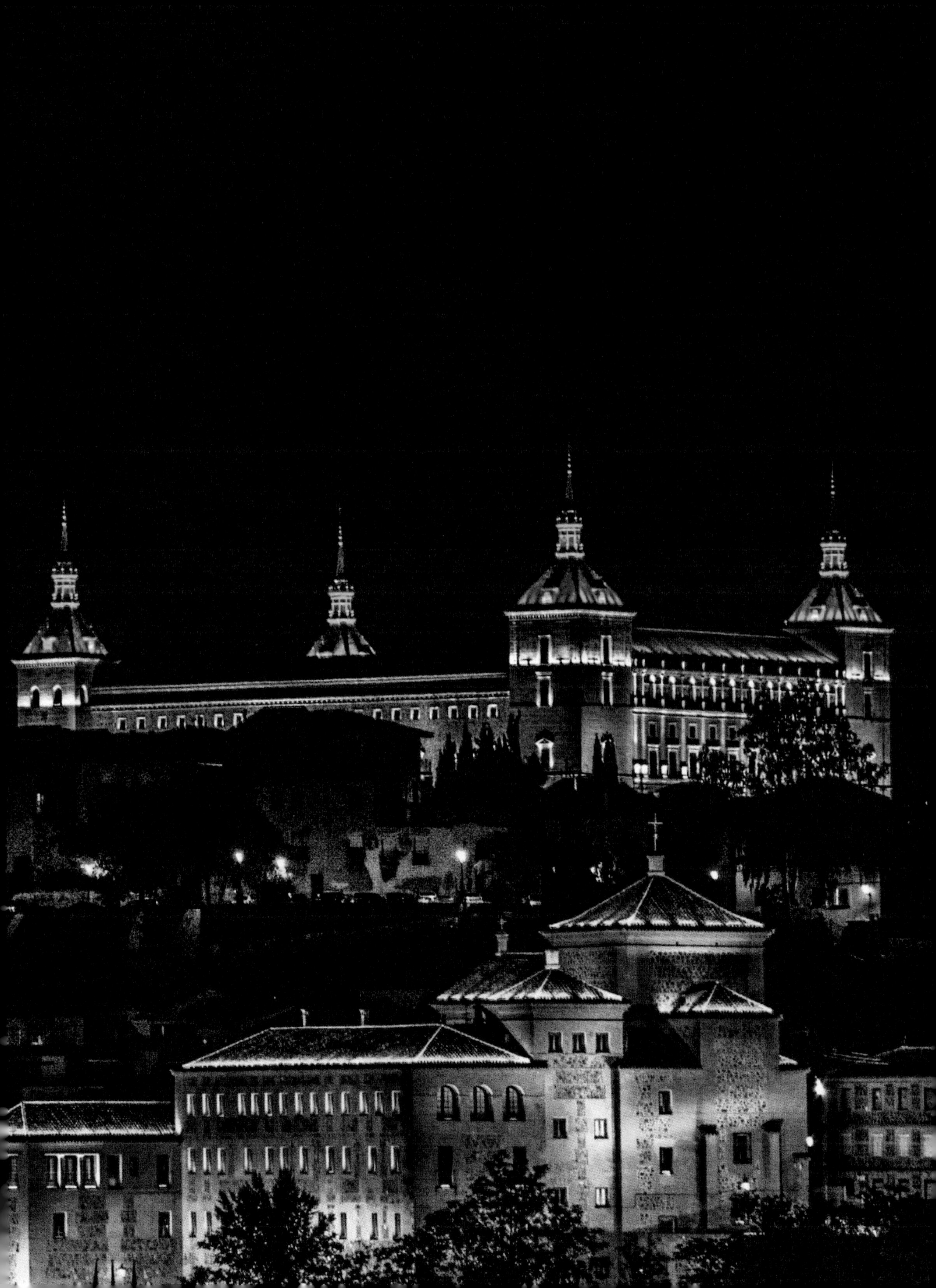

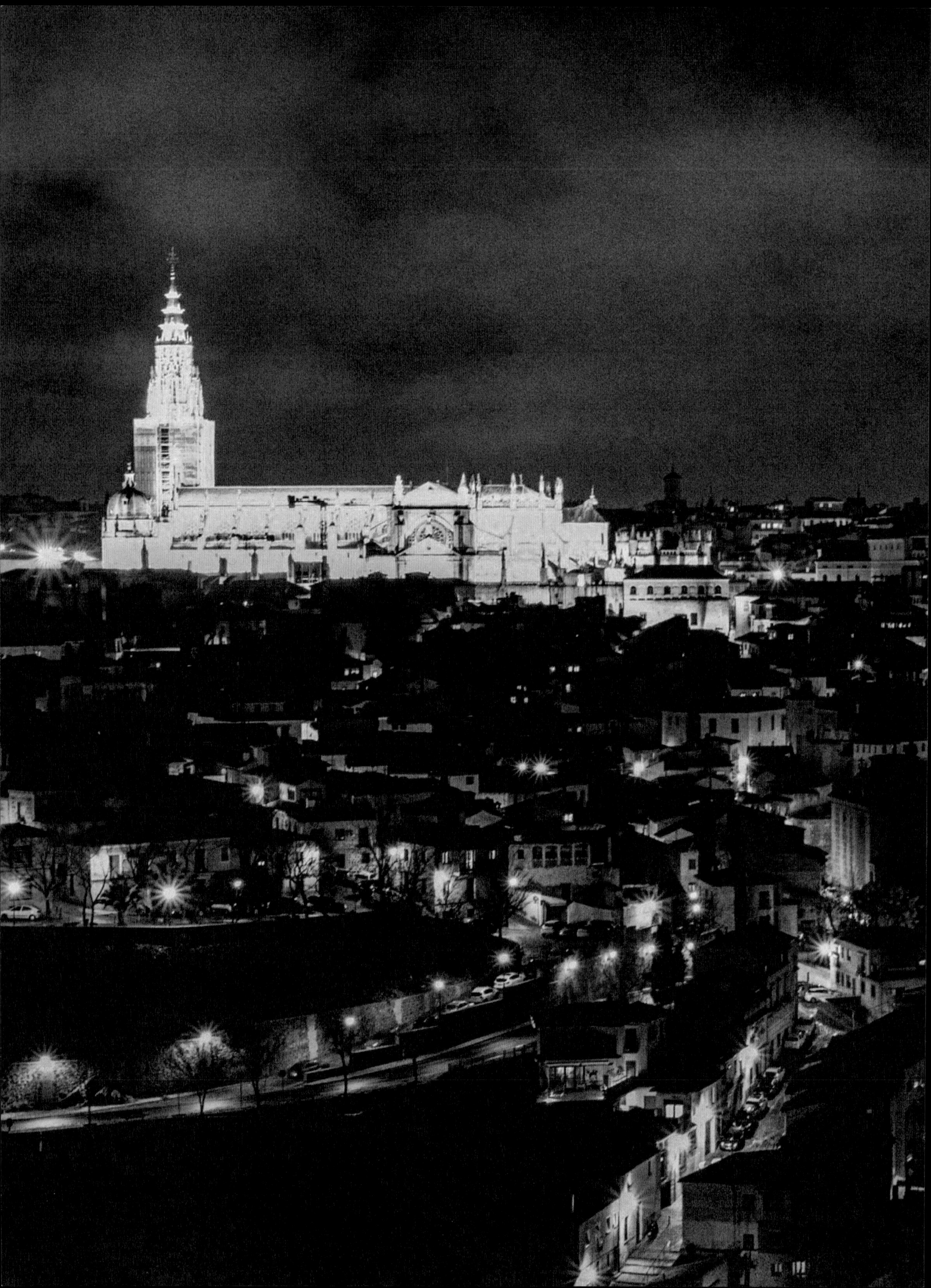

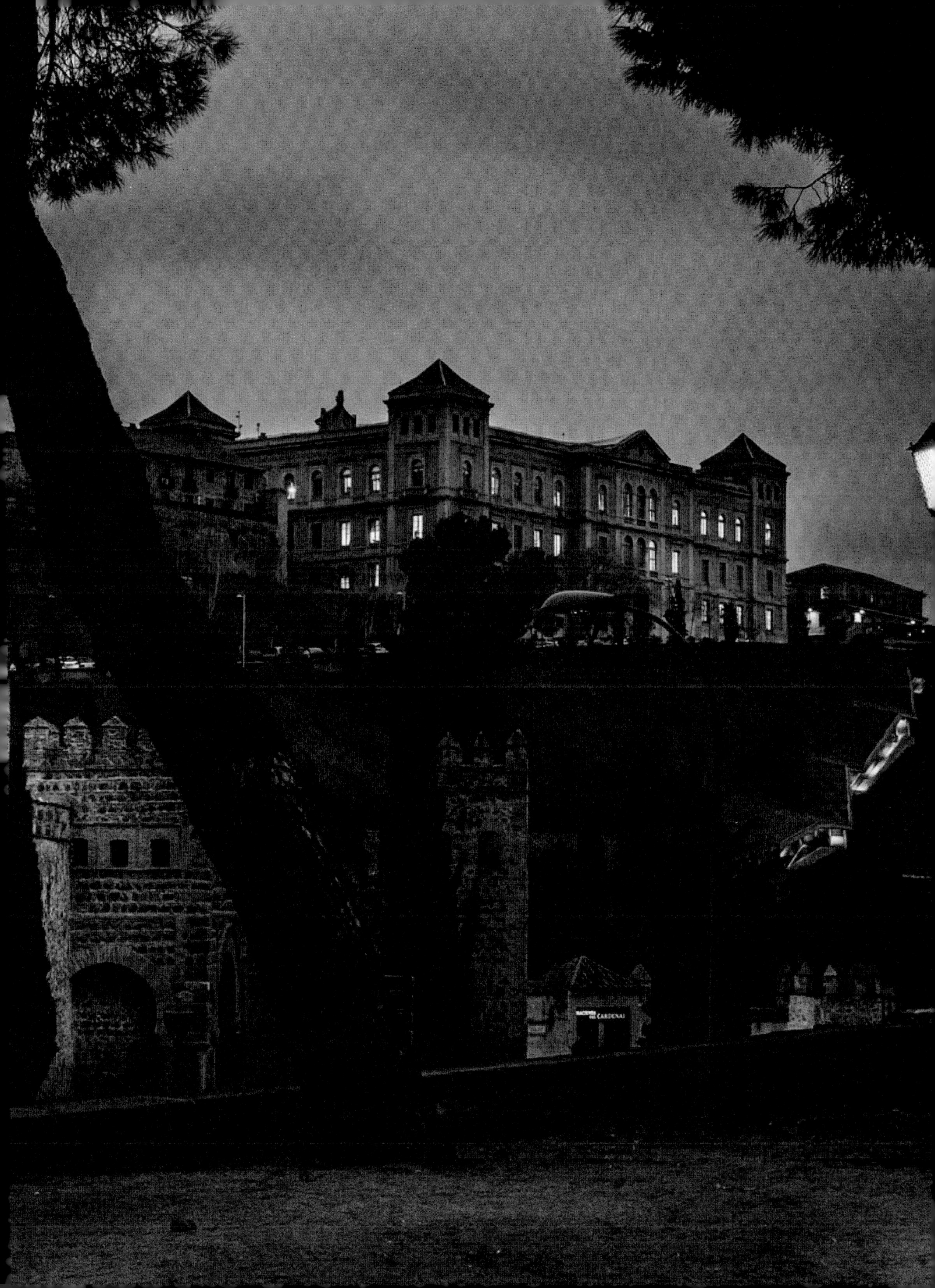

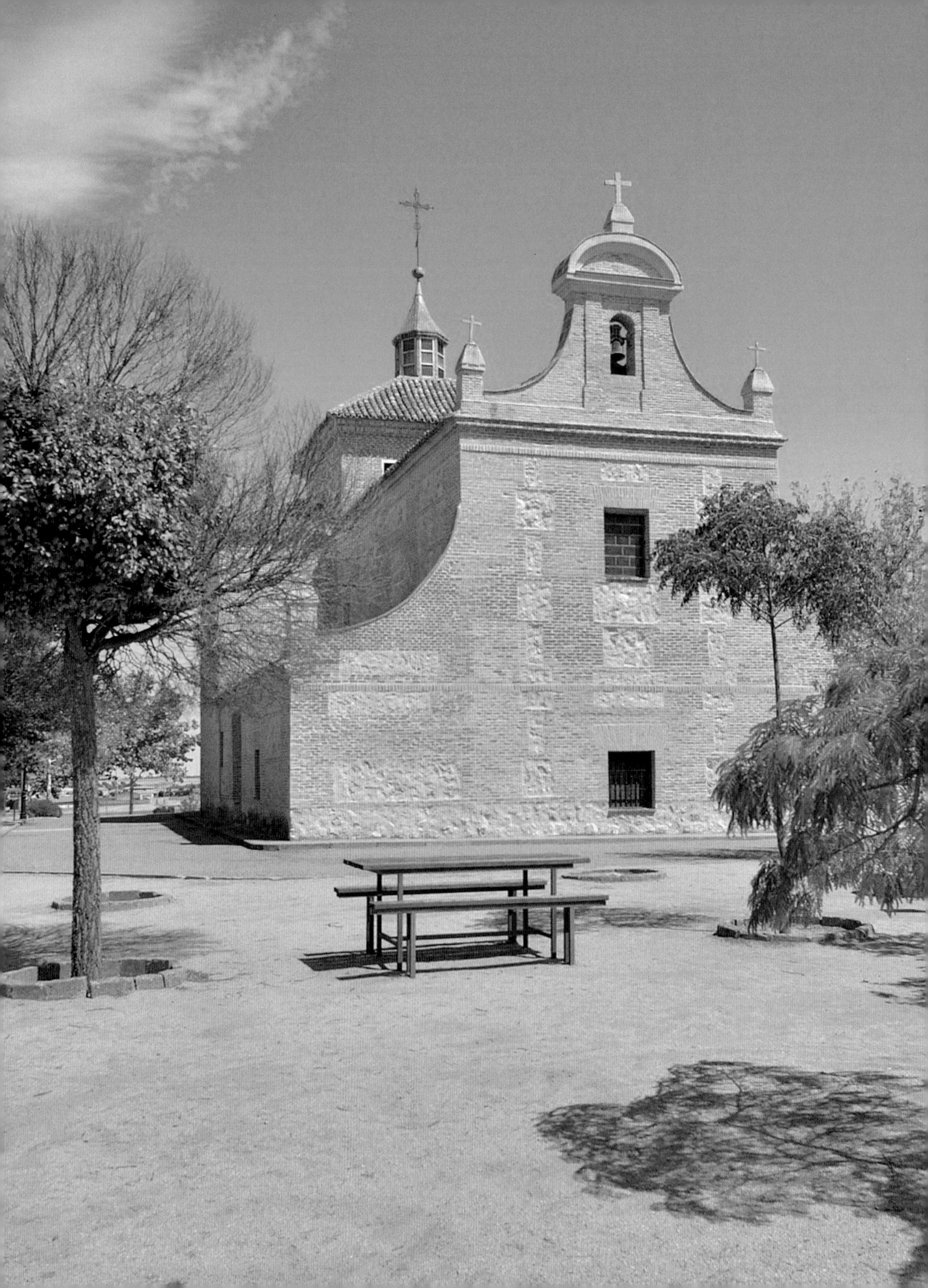

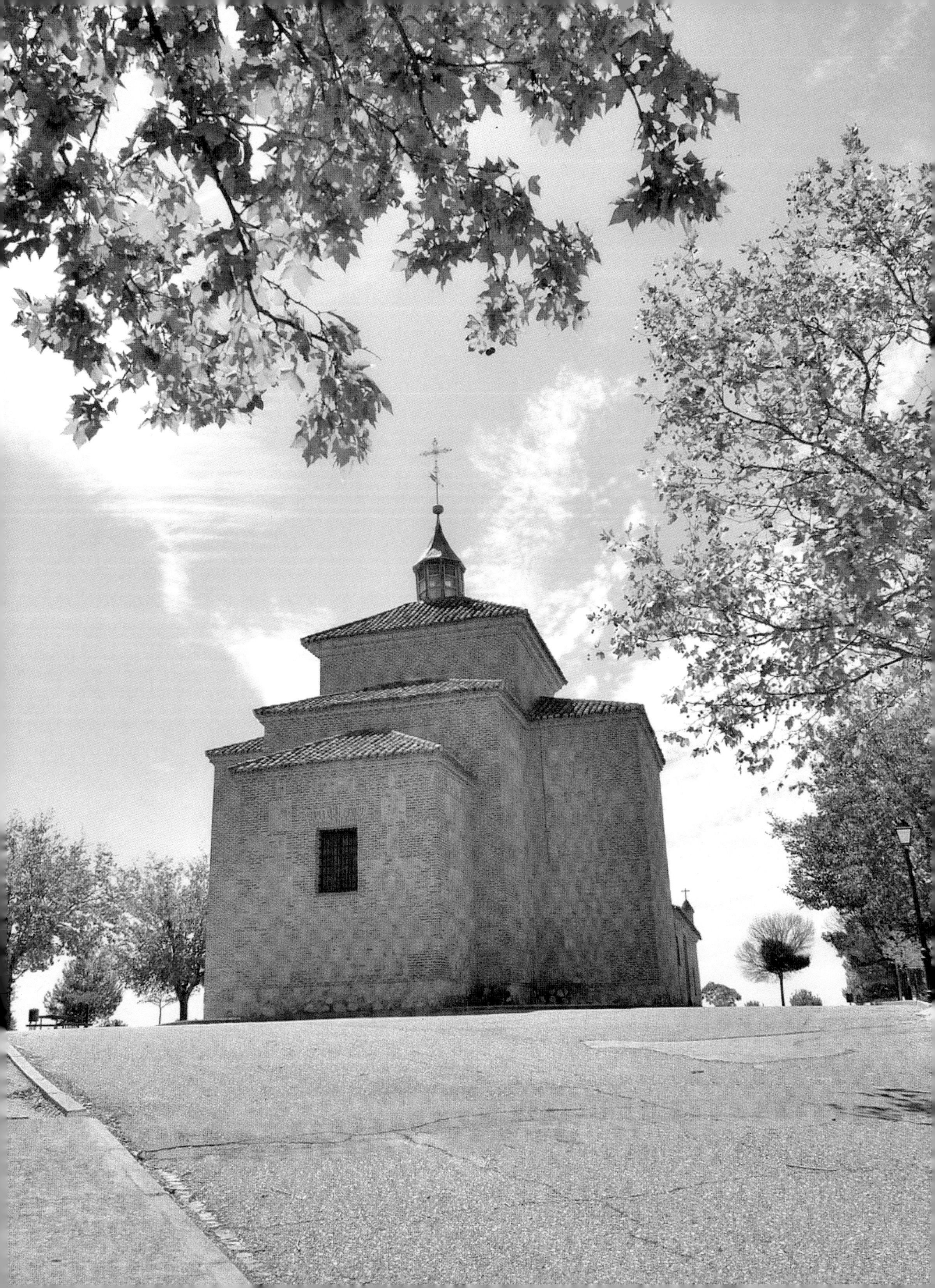

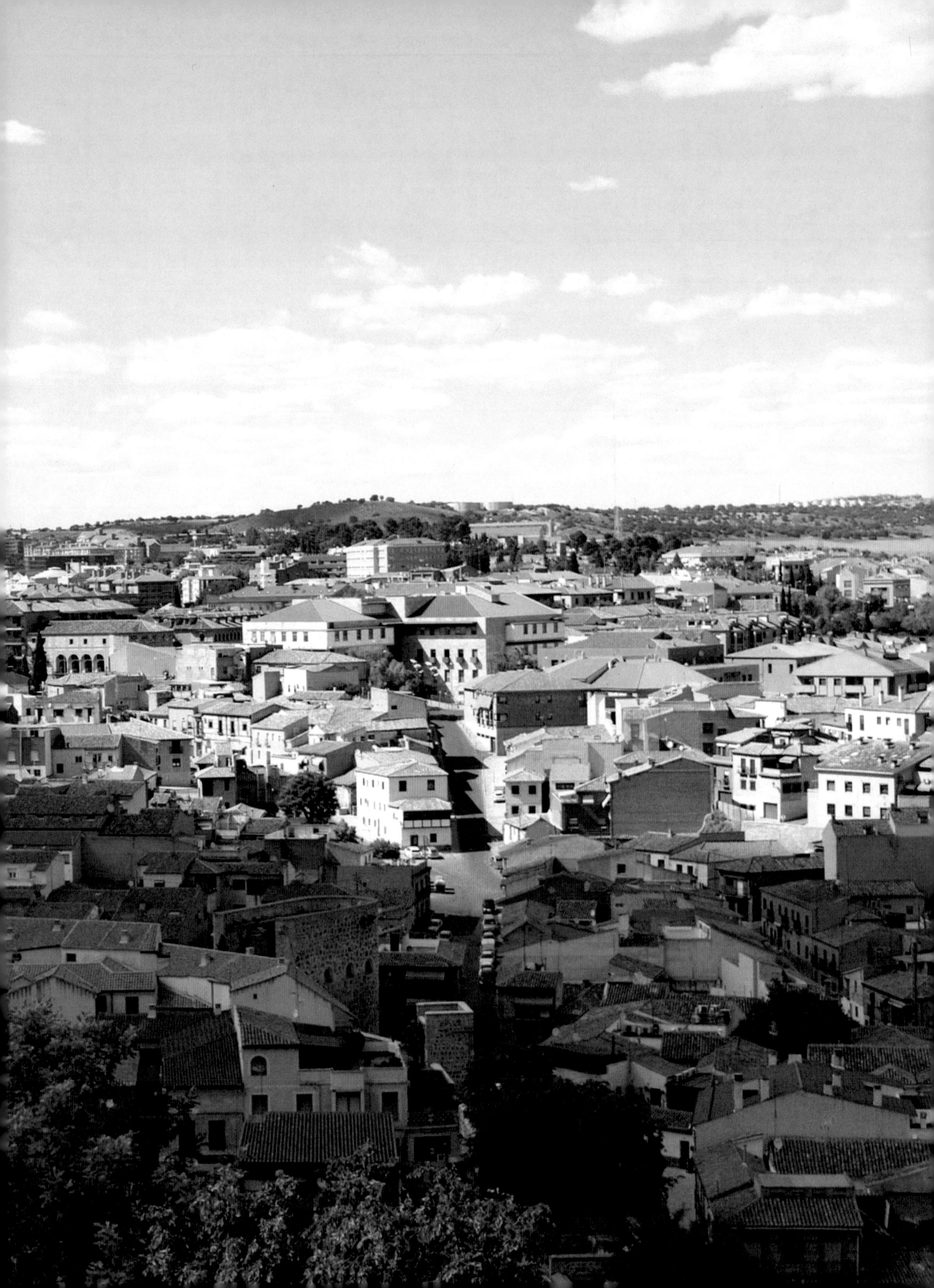

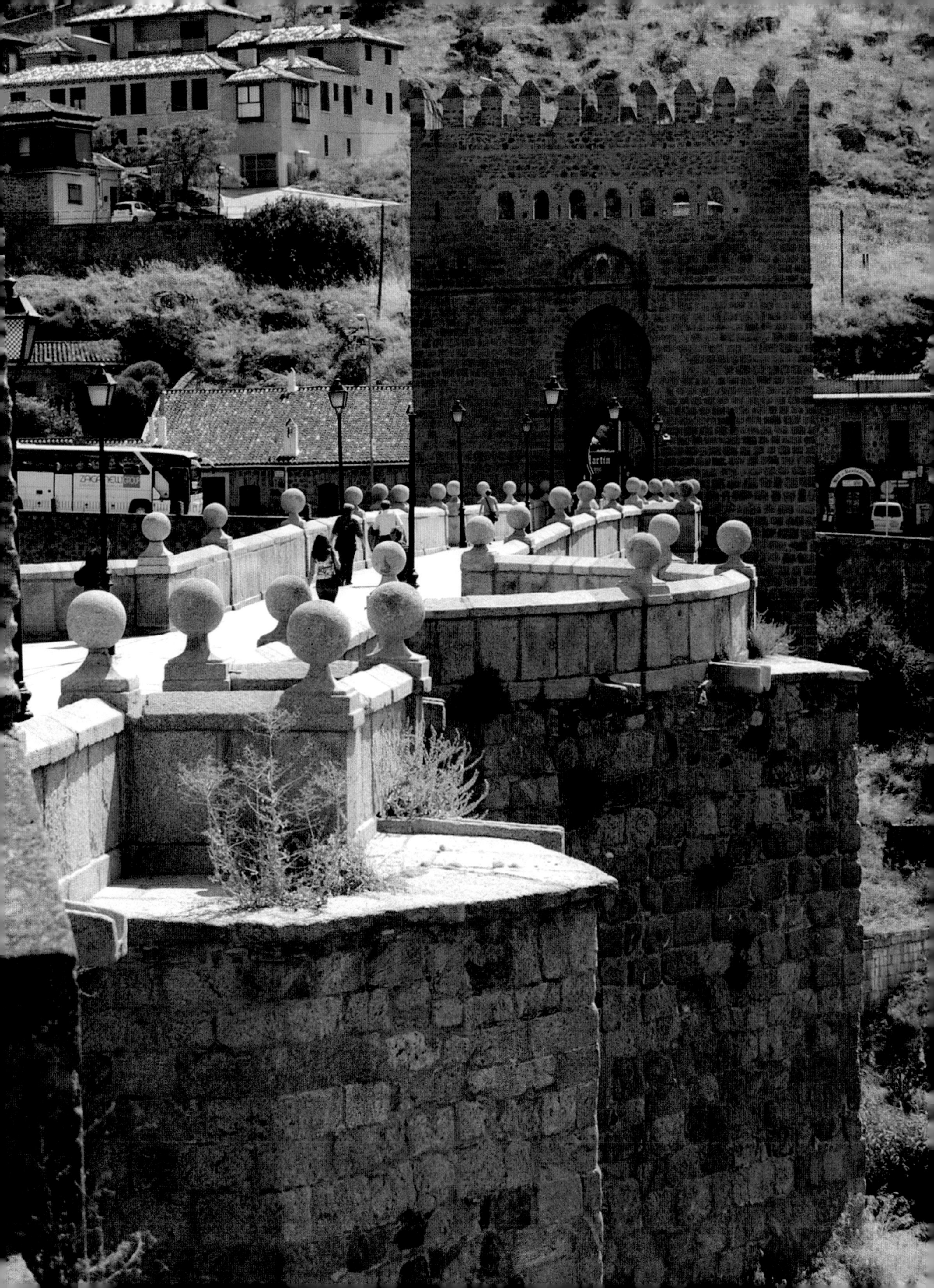

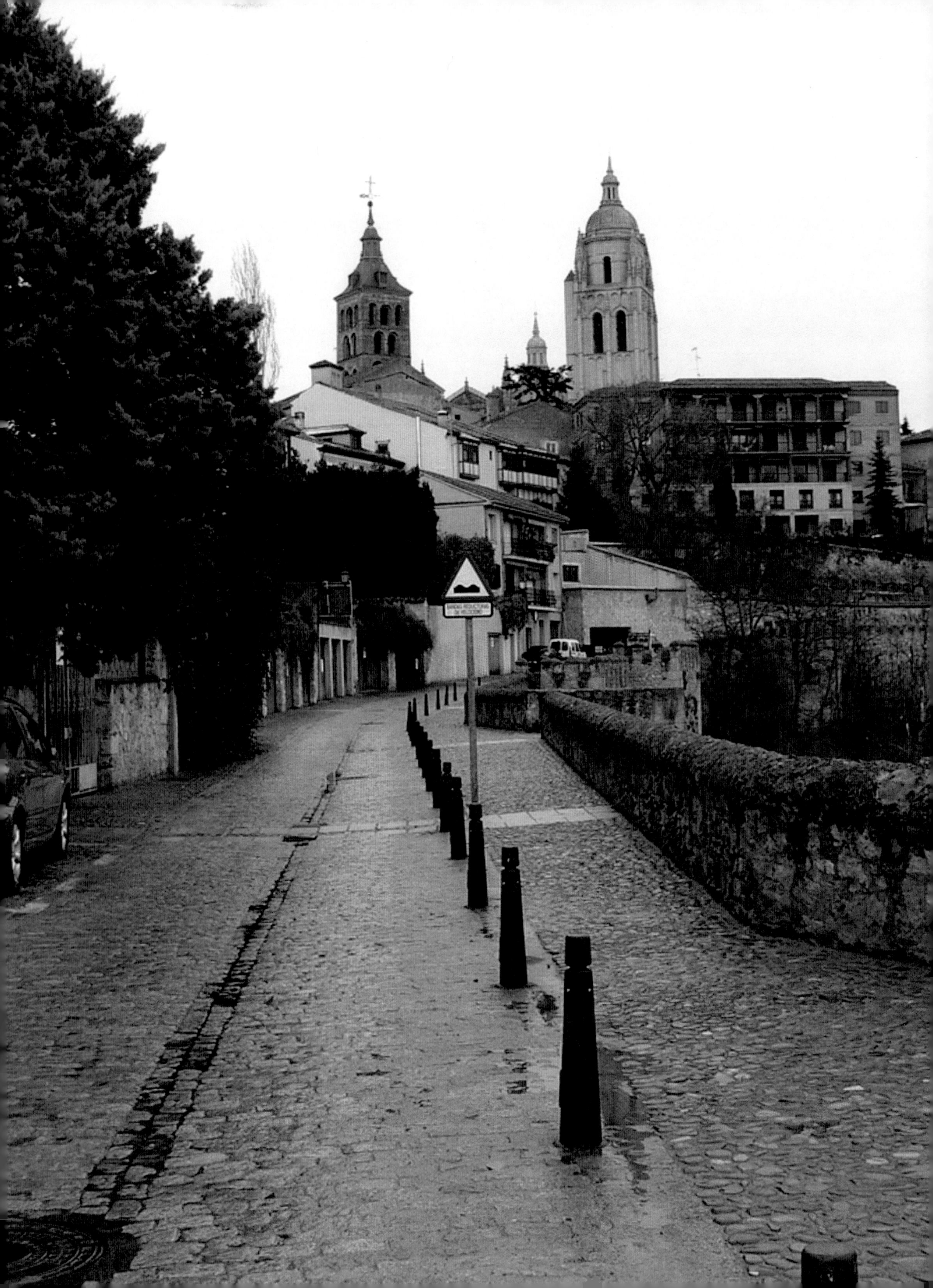

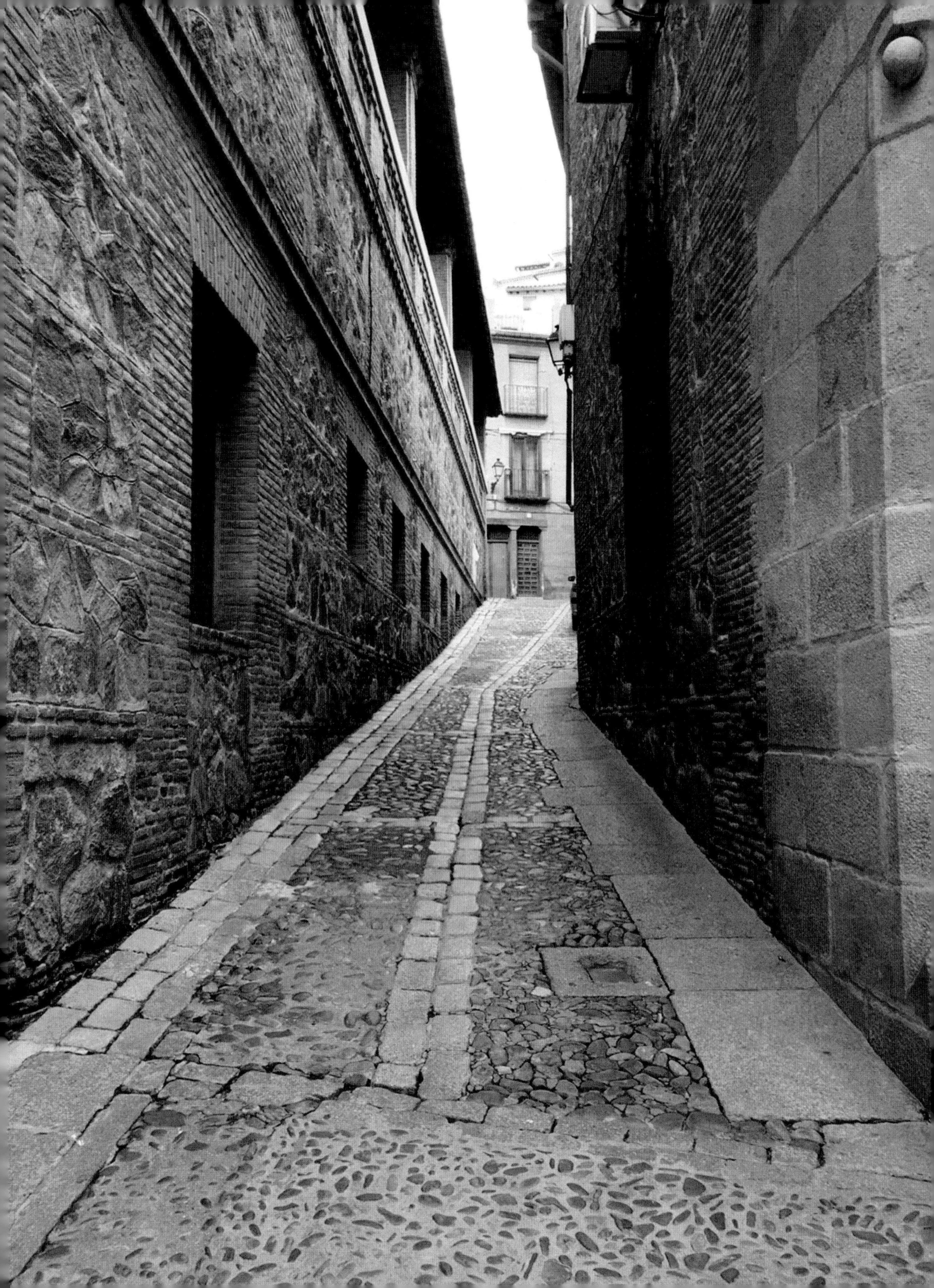

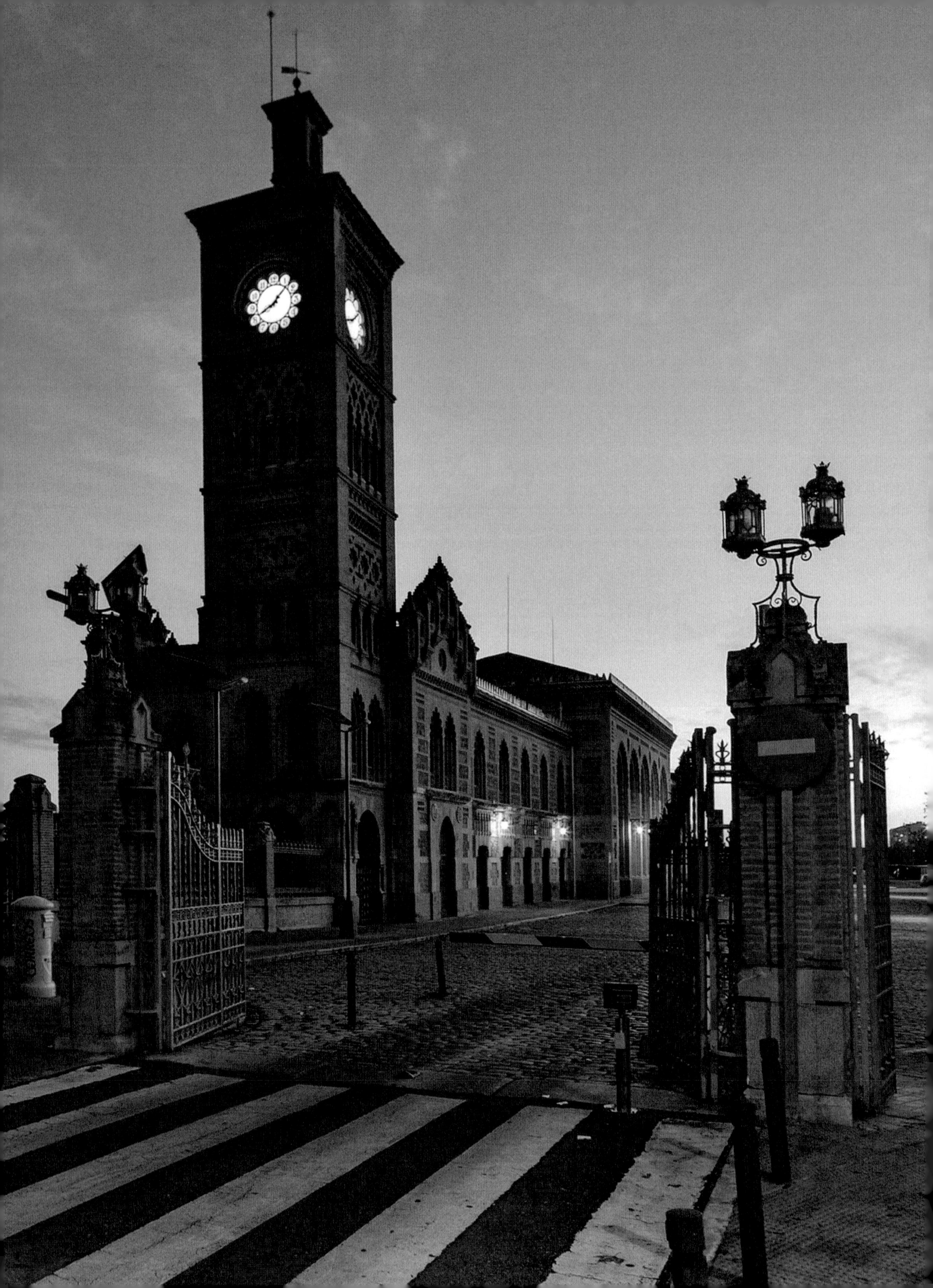

Made in the USA
Monee, IL
10 May 2022

96143817R00026